Fermentation

Fermentation

ÅSA SIMONSSON

How to make your own sauerkraut, kimchi, brine pickles, kefir, kombucha, vegan dairy, and more

LORENZ BOOKS

Contents

INTRODUCTION

As a child, I remember liking sauerkraut straight away, and we always had jars of it at home where it was a regular feature of our diet. Since then, fermented foods have been an important part of my life, both personally and professionally, and in this book, I hope to share with you some of the incredible health benefits that making and eating fermented foods can bring.

I was first introduced to fermentation and culturing as a young child by my Aunt Birgitta. A tumour on her hand disappeared after she started to eat lacto-fermented sauerkraut, and this miraculous-seeming experience started my aunt on her journey to becoming an organic farmer and one of the first commercial producers of lacto-fermented vegetables in Sweden.

I work as a nutritional therapist and a naturopath and also as a nurse, and I see many clients and patients in need of better health and indeed, a better diet. As you will find out in this book, fermented foods can be an important tool for achieving good health. I see in my job that unwell people tend to have under-functioning digestive systems. To be able to be truly healthy, our digestive system and gut need to be balanced and working well. If they're not, we are unable to assimilate the vital nutrients our food should provide for us, and we are also unable to properly eliminate toxins and waste products that our bodies no longer need. Fermented foods can be a highly effective path to a well-balanced digestive system and a way to enjoy greater health.

There are many other reasons to be excited about fermented foods, too: they are cheap and easy to make; they will introduce you to new and exotic flavours, aromas and textures; and fermentation is also a wonderfully creative form of food preparation. What could be more satisfying than lining up a row of brightly coloured jars, prepared by hand with love, and bursting with nutritional goodness?

Little did Aunt Birgitta know when she introduced me to fermented foods all those years ago that she would be such an inspiration as I started my own journey into healthy eating and fermentation. It has been amazing to have her as a mentor and I hope to pass on and share that with you. Happy fermenting!

Åsa

SAFETY NOTE

Fermentation is a natural process and results may vary; please read the first chapters carefully for general advice on ingredients, equipment, hygiene and safety.

Ferments and Cultures

All vegetables and fruits will mature and eventually start to rot. Fermenting and culturing are traditional ways of preserving food, which not only extend an ingredient's life and enhance its natural flavours, but have the significant benefit of making food more digestible.

In most countries, you will find some tradition of fermentation and the culturing of foods. Take for example beer in Germany, wine in France, sauerkraut in central and eastern Europe, kombucha in China (and Japan), kimchi in Korea, salami and olives in the Mediterranean, beans and grains in India, and kefir in Russia… in Sweden, where I am from, we love to ferment not only vegetables but also dairy and fish.

Below and right: Fermentation is regaining its rightful place within a healthy and balanced diet. Nutritionists and naturopaths alike are now prescribing fermented foods, and thanks to much exciting new research the health benefits are increasingly being recognised in mainstream healthcare.

Apart from preserving and enhancing the taste of food, the fermentation process increases the beneficial microorganisms that naturally live on our food, and regularly eating fermented foods is a highly effective way to improve nutrition, balance digestion and help gut health. Imagine preparing food in a way that not only preserves it, and enhances its taste and aroma, but also increases the quality, making it more digestible and its nutrients more bioavailable.

The terms 'wild fermenting' and 'culturing' are used intermittently in the world of fermentation. The difference between them is only slight. Wild fermenting is to ferment something without adding anything to help the process, apart perhaps from salt. Culturing is the adding of a culture or a starter to help the fermentation, with the intention of cultivating specific bacteria rather than just the ones naturally found on the vegetable. The ferment then becomes more controlled. A ferment recipe can be either wild or cultured, depending on whether you add a starter or culture. For example, to add whey in sauerkraut would be culturing rather than wild fermenting. If you add nothing but salt to your sauerkraut you are wild fermenting and not culturing.

Before telling you more about how to make the various fermented foods featured in this book I want to introduce you to a little bit of the history of fermentation as well as the science behind it.

Fermentation is a natural process that happens of its own accord in the right environment. Our knowledge of fermentation could be as old as the human race itself. We know that cabbage was fermented in China over 6000 years ago and that they prescribed fermented cabbage juice for various ailments and disease. In India at the same time cabbage salve was made and used for healing.

In Roman times the soldiers would take fermented foods on their long crusades. The Roman emperor Tiberius brought barrels of fermented foods on his journeys because his digestion benefited from it. Some of the earliest recipes found for fermented foods are from 50 BCE and written by the Roman scientist Plinius. The Romans loved their fermented foods and had two basic ways of preparing the ferment. One was to chop the vegetables small, packing them tightly with salt and leaving them in a sealed barrel, and the other way was to prepare a salty brine. The vegetables were always mixed with local herbs and wild plants. These ancient recipes, as you will see, sound very much like the ones we still use today.

In the Middle Ages, we know that fermented foods were widespread across Europe, though it wasn't until the 1700s that Captain Cook discovered that scurvy in sailors was preventable by bringing fermented cabbage in big barrels on long sailing trips for his crew. Vitamin C is stabilised during the fermentation process and this was a huge discovery in its time. Cook realised that certain foods – fermented foods as well as citrus fruit, fresh fruit and other vegetables – could provide the answer, and fermented cabbage had the advantage of lasting longer on the voyages. Recognised by the scientists of the period, Cook was hailed as the conqueror of the 'sea's great plague'.

Some countries have always enjoyed fermented and cultured foods as staple foods in their diet. In Japan, a macrobiotic diet is common, and includes various fermented soy products like miso, tempeh and tofu. A large amount of fermented vegetables is eaten through southeast Asia. Russian and Siberian food traditionally includes an array of fermented delights, such as kvass, borstjt, kapusta, kefir and yogurt.

Most societies all around the world have used or are still using some kind of fermentation; although the methods employed and the local ingredients that are fermented may be different, we all have the art of fermentation in common. And incredibly, even though this is something people have been doing for thousands of years, we have still not discovered a better natural, low-tech, safe and nutritious way of preserving our food.

Above: Evidence-based research tells us that a plant-based diet is the best for preventing serious digestive diseases. Plants give our gut not only probiotics from the lactic acid bacteria that live on all vegetables and fruits, but also prebiotics found in the fibre of vegetables and also legumes. If you ferment fresh vegetables and fruits you will increase the amount of probiotics in your diet even more.

Bacteria and Gut Bacteria

Bacteria are tiny single-cell organisms found pretty much everywhere. We believe that bacteria were the very first form of life here on earth and they thrive in diverse environments – the soil, in water, and also in humans. Bacteria come in many forms and can be distinguished by their different cell walls, their shape, or genetic makeup. Bacteria, like all other living organisms, need nutrients and water to survive. They can be aerobic, which means they need oxygen to survive, or anaerobic, when they do not need oxygen to survive. Some, facultative anaerobic bacteria, can live both with and without oxygen.

There are hundreds of different types of beneficial microorganisms living inside a healthy gut. Friendly bacteria are essential for a plethora of physical functions in our body. They communicate with and help white blood cells fight disease; they control the bad bacteria in the intestines, helping with bowel elimination; they provide important nutrients to the blood; they improve digestion; they manufacture several nutrients like B-vitamins; and are necessary for retaining a good level of vitamin B12 inside us.

Bacteria are named after the family they belong to as well as the type. For example, *Lactobacillus plantarum* is a group of bacteria that will increase during a vegetable fermentation process. Lactobacillus is the family of bacteria and plantarum is the specific type. This Lactobacillus family of bacteria, also called lactic acid bacteria, is the main bacteria involved in vegetable and fruit fermentation.

All bacteria in our intestine make up our gut microbiome or gut flora, and this flora should contain the right kind of bacteria in the right proportions. Our relationship with this microbiome is very complex indeed. Sometimes bacteria are vital for our well-being and sometimes they can cause disease and destruction. Our microbiome starts to develop in the womb – the placenta is itself a microbiome and a baby will get bacteria from this. Babies who have a natural vaginal birth pick up bacteria, and some mothers with babies born via a caesarean choose to bathe their newborn in vaginal fluid or swab their babies with vaginal bacteria to try and give them a natural environment for their microbiome to develop. Breastfeeding is also important for development of gut bacteria – the breast milk in itself will provide good bacteria, and so will the latching on to the mother's breast. This isn't a criticism if breasteeding is not possible but the research is interesting.

New studies are coming out continuously about our gut bacteria and how important they are. We have known for a long time that they help protect us from unwanted invaders in our gut as well as synthesising various vitamins like B-vitamins and vitamin K2. However, we are starting to realise that they do much more than this. Gut bacteria help regulate our body weight and glucose levels and help promote a normal metabolism. Studies show that bacteria actually control our hunger and cravings as well as how much energy we extract from the food we eat. This means that our microbiome can contribute to weight gain and weight loss. Experiments have been done where identical twins ate exactly the same diet and one put on weight whilst the other one didn't; the only difference between them was their microbiome.

Gut bacteria not only protect our gut from unwanted invaders, they can regulate and conduct our immune system. It is believed that at least 60% but probably as much as 80% of the immune system is in the gut, and a well-balanced microbiome means that your immune system is strong, and you are less likely to get ill and better able to heal any illnesses you might have. Allergies, asthma, eczema and auto-immune diseases such as coeliac, lupus and MS have increased dramatically over recent years, and the root causes could be, it is suggested, an over-stimulated or challenged immune system. Rebalancing your microbiome may help, and a way of doing this is to include fermented foods in your diet.

Gut bacteria helps convert the food we eat into certain hormones and chemicals, like serotonin and acetylcholine, that control our mood, appetite and general health. Changing your gut flora can have a positive effect on our mental health. Dr Natasha Campbell-McBride, a neurologist and nutritionist based in Cambridge UK, has had success in treating autism and learning disabilities, neurological disorders, psychological and psychiatric disorders, immune disorders and digestive disorders with her GAPS (gut and psychology syndrome) diet, in which fermented foods are a vital part.

In a nutshell, an ideal balance of good and bad bacteria in our microbiome in the gut forms the foundation for physical, mental, and emotional well-being. Feeding your own bacteria with other beneficial bacteria will have benefits for your general health and well-being, and including fermented foods is a fantastic and effortless way of doing this.

Below: The bacteria found on vegetables have over time formed a symbiotic relationship, particular to each other. When you ferment these vegetables, this relationship gets stronger. This is something that happens only in nature, and it is not possible to replicate this in a lab and put into a probiotic supplement. For this reason fermented vegetables are superior to probiotic supplements.

Above: One reason why the healthy bacteria in fermented foods are superior to a probiotic supplement is that the fermentation process allows the bacteria to slowly get used to the acidic environment of the ferment before it enters the stomach. The healthy bacteria in fermented red cabbage will survive the acidity of the stomach to reach the small intestine where it can do its magic. When you take a probiotic supplement, the healthy bacteria may not survive in the stomach or get to the next stage.

Lacto-fermentation

All fruits and vegetables are naturally covered with a layer of microorganisms. These microorganisms will start the fermentation process when the vegetable or fruit begin to break down. For this to happen, certain criteria also need to be fulfilled, such as the right temperature, the right amount of salt, and an anaerobic or oxygen-free environment. From a culinary point of view fermentation is an amazing way of preparing the food, changing its texture, and intensifying and enhancing its flavours and aroma. On top of this the nutritional value of the food will increase and it will become more digestible, helping us to feel good after a meal instead of too full and bloated.

Scientifically, lacto-fermentation is a spontaneous microbiological metabolic process where the microorganisms covering the vegetable will start to break down carbohydrates or sugars in the food and turn them into an organic acid, alcohol or gas. Vegetables and fruit are naturally high in lactic acid bacteria and these amazing little microbes, with the help from various enzymes, will turn the sugar in the vegetable or fruit into lactic acid. The various lactic acid bacteria thrive and multiply in the low pH of the lactic acid. The salt added to the ferment is also loved by the lactic acid bacteria. Luckily for both the lactic acid bacteria and for us, not many other bacteria like these conditions. The low pH and the salt, combined with the lactic acid bacteria itself, make it very hard for any other bacteria to grow here. Left on its own over time the lactic acid bacteria will start to ferment.

This lacto-fermentation happens in two stages. Firstly, a bacterium called Leuconostoc mesenteroides breaks down the sugars in the vegetables and starts to create the lactic acid, lowering the pH, and changing the environment inside the fermentation jar. This stage takes 3–7 days depending on the temperature of the surrounding environment and how much salt is being used. Preferably, at this stage the temperature should be around 18–20°C or 65–72°F. If it is warmer this stage will happen a bit quicker, and if colder a little slower. Salt will also slow down the fermentation process. The Leuconostoc mesenteriodes bacteria are heterofermentative, meaning they produce several products, the main one being lactic acid. The Leuconostoc mesenteroides is responsible for creating most of the unique taste of the fermented vegetables.

At the second stage the pH is so low that the Leuconostoc bacteria are less able to thrive and instead other lactic acid bacteria take over. Other products apart from bacteria are now being created, like acetylcholin, B-vitamins, vitamin K, and various enzymes. Lactobacillus plantarum, Lactobacillus curvatus and Lactobacillus brevis are a few examples of new bacteria entering the ferment at this second stage. These bacteria are homofermentative, meaning they produce only one thing, which is lactic acid. At this stage, the pH will be around 3.8 and can go down to as low as 3.4. In this acidic and salty environment, the lactic acid bacteria are pretty much the only bacteria that can survive. Despite having such a low pH, the ferment has no acidifying effect on the human body; when its broken down it actually has an alkalizing effect.

These two stages take approximately three weeks together for a vegetable ferment, depending on the variables such as temperature and salt, etc. It is recommended to leave the fermentation for at least three weeks to get the full benefit of as many various lactic acid bacteria as possible. Many people prefer to stop the ferment before this time, which is absolutely fine, but you should know that if you want all the incredible health benefits of fermented foods, as discussed later, it is recommended to ferment for the full two phases.

The level of vitamins and minerals in lacto-fermented food does not diminish and can even increase during the fermentation process. This amazing characteristic is not found in any other method of preparing food.

Despite the word 'lacto' the fermentation of vegetables has nothing to do with dairy. The bacteria was first discovered in dairy ferments, where it converted lactose into lactic acid, hence the original name. However, the bacteria found on vegetables convert other sugars, as there is no lactose in vegetables, fruts, nuts or grains. If you are lactose-intolerant you are still able to eat fermented vegetables.

Below: Brining vegetables is the oldest form of preservation, with a side helping of health benefits. Here are turnips, simply peeled, sliced and pickled in a salt water ferment.

Probiotics and Prebiotics

A probiotic food contains live bacteria or yeast with various health benefits; it is beneficial for replacing or supplementing damaged gut flora. Probiotics can be taken as a nutritional supplement, but of course fermented foods are an excellent source. Probiotic means 'for life', in contrast to the word antibiotic which means 'against life'.

Good bacteria, or probiotics, are only really helpful if they survive in the stomach and make it to the intestine. As the bacteria in the fermented food are used to an acidic environment already, they are very likely to survive in the stomach and make it to the small intestine. A probiotic supplement with beneficial gut bacteria does not always survive the acidic stomach environment. For this reason, traditionally fermented foods might fare better than commercial probiotic supplements, and this is indicated by some research. It's worth noting that if you heat your fermented foods up or use them in cooking, then you will kill most of these bacteria.

A prebiotic food is rich in a type of fibre, called oligosaccharides, that nourishes the good bacteria already in the gut. You could say it is a food for the probiotic. A probiotic introduces the bacteria, whilst the prebiotic fertilises the bacteria. Both are essential for good balance in the gut.

All foods with fibre contain some prebiotics, so vegetables do all have a certain amount. All fermented vegetables will have both probiotics and prebiotics present, which many commercial probiotic supplements do not. However, some vegetables are significantly higher in prebiotics, and including these in your ferments will be particularly beneficial for gut health. Foods high in prebiotics are spring onions or scallions, leeks, onions, chicory or Belgian endive, radishes, mooli or daikon, Jerusalem artichokes or sunchokes, asparagus, and dandelion leaves. Prebiotic foods are best eaten raw, so fermenting them is a great way of getting all their benefits.

Most of us have taken antibiotics at some point in our life. Antibiotics are life-saving medicines given to us when we have a bacterial infection and we really wouldn't want to be without this medicine. The problem with antibiotics is that they also kill many of our good bacteria. This will then have an adverse effect on the immune system, and we are more vulnerable to disease after we have taken a course of antibiotics. This can be less of a problem if good bacteria are introduced during and after taking antibiotics. Evidence-based research is now becoming available, and some dietitians and doctors are beginning to recommend taking probiotics after a course of antibiotics to replace or supplement damaged gut flora. Eating fermented foods is an amazing way to do this, and to improve our immune system.

Below: Homemade kimchi is full of probiotics and prebiotics, as well as being lower in salt than most bought versions. Strong in flavour, it can add a tasty boost to many dishes and is an easy and simple way of improving gut health. Kimchi is great on some freshly steamed pak choi.

Health Benefits of Ferments

Fermented foods have many health benefits to get excited about. Some are well-researched by scientists, and some are regular observations from my own experience.

It is important to remember that we are all different, and fermented foods will have different effects on different people. A very few people might find they are sensitive to fermented foods or have adverse reactions to them, something I will talk more about later. There are also differences between various fermented foods. The best way to be certain that you are consuming healthy fermented foods is to make them yourself. Some shop-brought products are very processed and may contain huge amounts of refined cooking salt – these are not healthy and I do not recommend you eat them. Pasteurised sauerkraut does not contain the healthy bacteria found in the homemade products, although they can still be a good food, and many commercial yogurts tested do not contain sufficient amounts of healthy bacteria to have the benefits we are after. The heavily promoted sugary pasteurised probiotic 'health' drinks you find on supermarket shelves will not do much for your gut flora. Evidence of this is demonstrated in a very interesting small study carried out by the BBC in the UK, on 30 people divided into three groups. For four weeks, group one was given an 'off the shelf' probiotic yogurt drink to take daily; group two drank kefir, a fermented unpasteurised dairy drink; and group three were instructed to

Below: Fresh vegetables are packed full of beneficial vitamins and minerals, and the process of fermentation captures these nutrients rather than destroying them.

eat foods high in prebiotics. Apart from this they were all following their usual diet. Their gut bacteria were tested before and after the four weeks. The result surprised the researchers. Group one didn't show any significant increase in healthy bacteria, which tells us that these popular probiotic drinks can be a waste of money. Group three had a significant increase in a type of bacteria called Feacalibacterium. These bacteria help produce a substance called butyrate which helps feed the colon and is very good for inflammatory bowel diseases. Group two, however, had the biggest change of all the groups. They saw a rise in a whole range of Lactobacillus, known to be very good for gut health and for helping food intolerances. This was so mind-blowing for the researchers that they decided to look into fermented foods a bit more. They did some testing on various fermented foods, including traditionally homemade fermented foods that had not been pasteurised as well as some off-the-shelf versions from supermarkets. The study showed that the homemade fermented foods had several strains of beneficial bacteria whilst the shop-bought pasteurised foods had very little or none at all. So, in a nutshell, eating homemade fermented foods, including kefir and sauerkraut, may greatly enhance your gut health whilst bought fermented foods might not be as good value.

I should emphasise that fermented foods will not 'cure' all your diseases and ailments. However, including fermented foods in a diet may improve everyone's health. These are several possible health benefits seen when eating live cultured and fermented foods.

Below: The bigger the range of fermented foods and drinks you try, the more kinds of beneficial bacteria you will ingest. A fermented yogurt with brined cucumbers is a double-hit of goodness.

Eating fermented foods will promote the friendly intestinal bacteria in your gut. The ferment is full of both probiotics and prebiotics and these will supply your microbiome with the food it needs for proper balance to be restored in the gut. The more varied the kind of vegetables you use, the more different kinds of probiotic and prebiotic strains you will find.

Fermenting makes the food more digestible and more bioavailable. This is happening because the food becomes pre-digested when it is fermented. There are also a lot of enzymes formed during the fermentation process that help digest other foods you eat with your fermented food. You could say that fermented foods work as a digestive enzyme.

The fermentation process itself will generate and increase the level of several nutrients: B-vitamins and, especially, B12 and an active form of folic acid. Fermentation produces K2, a vitamin essential for your heart and cardiovascular health, and one not easily taken up from other foods. Any omega 3 essential fatty acid in the food will increase. The quality of vitamin C is also increased and preserved in the food. In contrast, most other methods of food preparation are found to deplete the levels of vitamin C in the ingredients.

The generation of B12 is particularly interesting. Most of my clients are low in B12 and it doesn't seem to make any difference if they are vegans or not (B12 is found only in animal products). A healthy microbiome is supposed to synthesise its own B12 but this is not happening properly if the microbiome is not balanced. By adding ferments to your diet, you will balance the microbiome and be able to create your own B12, as well as introduce the active and bioavailable B12 within the food.

Live fermented and cultured foods work as a potent detoxifier. Fermented foods are great chelators, which means they are excellent at drawing out heavy metals and a large number of other toxins. For this reason, you may find you experience some adverse detox symptoms at first, if you are introducing too many fermented foods at once.

The fermentation process will help to get rid of naturally-occurring as well as added toxins. Some foods contain natural toxins and anti-nutrients – such as phytic acid and lectins, which are found in all grains, legumes, nuts and seeds. These bind minerals such as iron and zinc, and can make them unavailable for absorption. Fermentation lowers these anti-nutrients to a much better level. Nitrates and oxalic acid in foods are reduced by fermentation, and research has also shown that the fermentation process will help get rid of added toxins like some herbicides and pesticides. This suggests that non-organic foods are better eaten fermented than non-fermented.

Above: Making ferments will become an everyday part of your routine. An hour here and there preparing and potting the vegetables, and you'll have a regular store of ferments of all kinds just ready and waiting.

Fermented foods can help with the uptake of minerals, especially iron and also zinc, magnesium, calcium and iodine.

Ferments are excellent for optimising your immune system, as at least 80% of our immune system is situated in our gut.

Ferments help with the production and balancing of stomach acid; they are good both when stomach acid is too low, as they increase the acidity in the stomach, and good for when it is too high, as they help protect the lining of the stomach and intestine.

Fermentation helps the body to produce acetylcholine. Acetylcholine is a neurotransmitter associated with the parasympathetic nervous system that is all about relieving stress, rest and digestion, feeling content and calm and enhancing your moods.

Fermentation may help to stop bloating, gases and prevent constipation; it may also help in calming diarrhoea.

Fermentation helps with the creation of short-chained fatty acids that help protect the lining of our gut, which improves conditions like leaky gut, food allergies, candida albicans, and other digestive disorders. Short-chained fatty acids are also involved in the body's energy production.

Fermented foods may help to balance blood sugar levels and improve insulin sensitivity, and can lower the GI and GL of the meal you are having with the ferment. Balanced blood sugar levels are vital for good health. GI and GL are abbreviations for glycaemic index and glycaemic load, which indicates the food's effect on the blood sugar. The higher the GI level of the food is, the higher the level of glucose in the blood. Insulin sensitivity is associated with diabetes, low energy, depression, irritability, poor concentration, cravings, difficulty losing weight, brain fog and insomnia. Fermented foods can help rebalance GI and GL, and will reduce your cravings for sugary snacks.

When Ferments can Help

The father of Medicine, Hippocrates, believed that all disease starts in the gut, and this is what most naturopaths believe still today. I would dare to say that at least 90% of clients coming to me have their root cause of their disorder in an unbalanced gut.The following are some conditions that may be helped by balancing and enhancing our microbiome. We should be wary of treating serious diseases simply, and to view fermented food as a catch-all remedy, but it is undeniable that regularly including fermented foods will help us to balance and enhance our all-important microbiome.

Constipation and diarrhoea: Fermented foods can be helpful in the relief of both constipation and diarrhoea as well as helping with IBS. I have found that fermented drinks like milk kefir and kefir water are particularly good for this, but any fermented food will introduce good bacteria into the gut to start the healing process. There are many causes for constipation and diarrhoea so this cannot be seen as a diagnosis or cure-all but it is a useful tool in my experience.

Leaky gut: Many clients that come to me suffer from a leaky gut or intestinal hyperpermeability. This is a condition that is not recognised by most medical doctors, and many think this is an imaginary condition made up by complementary therapists. However, there is now evidence that this is a real condition, where the lining in the small intestine is damaged, and toxins, food and bacteria leak into the bloodstream. Leaky gut is

Below: Personally I avoid buying fermented foods as you don't always know how much salt they have used. When selling krauts one needs to be very careful with hygiene and for this reason, I believe that many of the commercial ferments may have had too much salt added for them to be healthy in the long run. Making your own allows you to control the level of salt used.

characterised by bloating, gases, pains, food sensitivities, cramps, tiredness and 'brainfog'. Leaky gut can lead to other digestive disorders and there is a belief that it could be a root cause of many modern diseases including autoimmune disease. There are functional medicine tests for leaky gut that can be organised by a Nutritional Therapist or Naturopath.

Heartburn and reflux: Heartburn is believed to be caused by too much acid in the stomach. However, heartburn can also be caused by too little – when there is not enough acid in the stomach the foods eaten are not broken down properly and can start to ferment, creating gases that, together with some stomach acid, can come back through the sphincter to the oesophagus and cause burn or pain. If there is too little stomach acid, fermented foods can help to make the stomach more acidic; if there is too much, they will help protect the stomach lining.

Food allergies: Many, many of my clients' food allergies have been relieved by healing their gut. Fermented foods are an important part of this.

High cholesterol: Some studies have shown that fermented foods may help reduce cholesterol.

Depression: The gut is connected to the brain via the vagus nerve, the enteric nervous system, and the gut-brain axis. Several studies indicate that good gut health and a balanced microbiome may help with depression, anxiety and other psychological disorders. Most of our serotonin is created in the gut, and the more balanced the microbiome, the more serotonin.

Diabetes: According to recent studies the microbiome of a diabetic person differs from someone without diabetes. This indicates that type 2 diabetes can be linked to the microbiome balance. Eating a healthy wholefood diet including ferments is a great way of balancing your intestinal microbiome.

Coeliac and other autoimmune disease: Autoimmune diseases are on the increase. Autoimmune disease is a result of an overactive immune system. Chrohn's disease and ulcerative colitis are examples of autoimmune diseases of the digestive system. As a large part of our immune system sits in our gut it is considered likely by many health professionals that there could be gut problems, and healing the gut would be part of their protocol for someone with an autoimmune disease. Eating fermented foods will not cure any autoimmune disease, but it may help to rebalance the microbiome in your gut which then may help an overactive immune system. It is important to consult a health professional before you embark on huge diet changes though, and to take small steps in the beginning.

GAPS diet and autism: It is beyond the scope of this book, but I should mention the GAPS (gut and psychology syndrome) diet developed by Dr Natasha Campbell-McBride, which has treated thousands of children and adults with autism using her programme based on reducing certain carbohydrates and introducing fermented foods.

Above: Fermented foods have a very special scent. I love the smell of fermented cabbage, but many people do not. It is an acquired scent and I am sure you will learn to love it, just like the taste. It does not taste the way it smells, so do not let the fragrance put you off! I have had people coming to my workshops telling me that they can't stand ferments, but that they have heard they are good for you. Most of these people leave my workshops loving fermented foods.

When to Avoid Ferments

It is not common, but some people do not react well to fermented foods – I have had a few clients who cannot eat fermented foods without getting bad digestive symptoms. These are a few possible causes to consider:

Fungus and yeast: Some people have concerns that fungus and yeast could contaminate the ferment. Some health authorities suggest that any fermentation that includes yeast should be avoided. It is your decision, but my view is that if you ferment your vegetables with salt in a clean or sterilised jar, and are careful with hygiene in general (as we always should be when we are working with foods), as well as making sure the process happens in an anaerobic environment, this should not be a problem at all. Remember that few bacteria, apart from the lactic acid bacteria we are after, like the naturally acidic and salty environment of fermentation. If you are worried, you could use a little bit of probiotic powder in your vegetable ferments as a starter. This controls the ferment, in that the bacteria in the probiotic powder is the main bacteria that will grow. I don't add probiotic powder to my general ferments, but many people decide to do this.

Histamine sensitivity: Fermented foods are high in histamine. This is a neurotransmitter and is known for causing an immediate inflammatory response in our immune system. It causes the blood vessels to dilate so that white blood cells can find and attack the infection or problem – which is, of course, what they are supposed to do. However, if you cannot break down histamine properly, you might develop an intolerance. Because histamine travels in the bloodstream it can cause symptoms anywhere in the body. Common histamine intolerance symptoms are migraines, sleep problems, high blood pressure, hives, itchiness, congestion and abdominal pain Histamine is broken down by enzymes but histamine-sensitive people are often lacking in these enzymes. This can sometimes be for genetic reasons but more often not; there can be many reasons as to why these enzymes are lacking and it is not always easy to find out why. Non-genetic reasons for histamine sensitivity could be a leaky gut, intestinal bleeding and small-intestine bacterial overgrowth (SIBO), hormonal imbalances and allergies. Histamine-sensitive people should avoid ferments. If you suspect you have a histamine imbalance, do consult a health professional.

Bloating and discomfort: For anyone new to fermented foods you should start with a small amount and then gradually increase, to let your digestive system get used to it. If you have a sensitive digestive system you might otherwise find you have gas, bloating and discomfort. This will ease off when your digestive system gets accustomed to all the new healthy bacteria. However, if you have severe digestive issues you might find that fermented foods will be a challenge even if you are moderate with your intake. Do seek a health professional's advice as it might be best to avoid fermented foods until your digestive health is better.

Underactive thyroid: If you have an underactive thyroid you might have heard that you should stay away from cabbage and the rest of the brassica family. It is true that brassicas contain goitrogens that can inhibit the thyroid from synthesising thyroid hormones, but if you cook or ferment brassicas most of the goitrogens will be destroyed in the process. If you are worried, however, you can choose other vegetables to ferment.

Right: There is a lot of sometimes conflicting dietary and health advice available that can confuse, even for a nutritionist. Although we all have a similar biology we are all individuals. What is good for your friend might not be good for you. My advice is that if you think certain foods are not good for you, then take them out of your diet for a while and only slowly reintroduce them. If you find you get unpleasant symptoms again then take them out for a longer period to see if your condition improves.

Using Ferments

So, how are you going to get these amazing probiotic foods into your diet and enjoy all of their health benefits. I often get asked how much to eat or if there is a upper limit to what you should eat in a day. My suggestion is, in the beginning, to eat a few tablespoons of fermented vegetables with each meal. If you get any digestive symptoms like bloatedness or any pain, then start off with a little bit less and slowly increase as you get used to the fermented foods. Similarly, start with a glass of fermented drink per day and if your digestive system agrees with this you can drink more.

Ferments can be enjoyed on their own but are best with other foods; they can be great condiments and work as a digestive aid. I add fermented foods to most of my dishes, and what I use mainly depends on what I have in the fridge. Any salad, soup, casserole or curry I create will also have a bit of sauerkraut or kimchi added before serving.

Fermented foods are wonderful to add in cooking. If you notice that your kimchi or sauerkraut is starting to go off or if you don't like the texture of the kraut you just made, then you can use it in cooking, where it will add a sour umami flavour to your food. It has to be noted that heating ferments will sadly remove their probiotic health benefits, but they still offer a nutritious vitamin- and mineral-rich ingredient. Personally, I think kimchi especially lends itself to be used in cooking, and sauerkraut is of course traditionally used in cooking in Germany, Poland and other eastern European countries, especially with meat dishes.

Below left to right: Add a spoon of kimchi to your soup for a health boost and beautiful umami flavour. Fermented berry jam works well with many desserts and is particularly delicious with rice pudding. Sauerkraut stirred into a stew is traditional in Eastern Europe and an easy way to get the benefits of fermented foods.

BREAKFASTS

For a quick breakfast add some dairy kefir in your normal smoothie for probiotic benefits and protein. What about some coconut or dairy kefir or yogurt with your granola, topping it up with homemade fermented 'queen's jam'. Or try porridge with the pear chutney – it's like they are made for each other. A poached or fried egg with my fresh turmeric sauerkraut and

half an avocado is an awesome breakfast containing good protein, healthy fats, vitamins, antioxidants, minerals and probiotics. Kimchi or sauerkraut pancakes are another favourite for brunch on a lazy morning.

Above: Adding fermented veggies to raw leaves will take your salad to another level in terms of both flavour and health benefits.

DRINKS

It is great to start the day with a glass of kefir water, especially on an empty stomach so that the little bacteria go straight to your small intestine where they do all their good work. I often drink this instead of water and also add it as the liquid element to my smoothies. Fermented drinks are, I find, a great option for people who do not like fermented foods; most children enjoy water kefir. And, fermented drinks can work wonders for an upset stomach pretty instantly.

SALADS AND SANDWICHES

Sauerkraut is perfect as part of a sandwich filling, adding nutritious crunch and flavour, and to make it more digestible. And salads without sauerkraut are missing something in my opinion. These are great ways to first introduce sauerkraut to someone that is not a fermented food convert already. Start with a little bit if you are not sure and add more when you get used to the different tastes. The juice from your sauerkraut, kimchi or pickles can also be used in a salad dressing. You never have to waste any of your ferment.

MEAT DISHES

Most meat dishes benefit from added sauerkraut. Not only do they usually go beautifully together taste-wise, but the sauerkraut (or pickle or kimchi) also makes it easier for you to digest the meat. Hot dogs, burgers and barbecues are taken to another level with added sauerkraut or kimchi.

PUDDINGS

Fermented foods are a great blood sugar balancer and will very quickly get rid of your sugar cravings. Homemade yogurt with fermented jam and topped with some granola is both healthy and delicious. Serve your favourite cake recipe with a fermented chutney 'jam'. And my raw nut chocolate cheesecake is very good!

Below: Fermented drinks are almost too good to be true. Instead of sugary soft drinks, try water kefir, kombucha or one of the other fermented drinks.

CHAPTER ONE:

Getting Started

'dry-salt ferment' means you do not add any water or brine and use only the water contained in the vegetables themselves. The second method is the 'brine ferment', which has salty water added to the vegetables.

Fermented vegetables, lacto-fermented vegetables or sauerkraut are the most common names people use, but they are basically referring to the same thing. Humans all over the world ferment vegetables, and have done so for thousands of years, although in a lot of Western countries the art has, surprisingly, been forgotten. Many people I teach have never even heard of it. As it was used in the past for preserving food, the practice diminished after the arrival of the wonderful fridge and freezer. In our modern society, we also don't like to wait around for things, so the thought of not eating what you make for the next three or so weeks might be an odd concept. However, now more is known about its health benefits, fermentation is becoming fashionable and mainstream again.

Fermented vegetables have an intense, deep, sour and salty flavour. Most adult people love the taste and texture straight away, though for some it can be more of an acquired taste; in my experience the more you eat it the more you will that loves it and another that doesn't.

One of the reasons we love fermented foods is their umami flavour. Umami is called the fifth taste, together with sweet, salty, sour and bitter; it can perhaps best be translated from the Japanese as a deliciously pleasant and moreish savoury taste.

Fermenting vegetables is seriously easy to do. The hardest thing for most people is to wait for them to get ready. For me, this is part of the beauty of fermenting. Rarely do we wait for anything any more. We are used to having things straight away or we get restless, bored or agitated. I like to see fermentation as a practice of self-discipline. You can't stop thinking of how they are going to turn out and it can feel a bit frustrating not being able to eat it straight away. Then, you forget about it and so it's really exciting when it is ready and you get to finally enjoy your creation.

Before you begin, it is important to read the preceding sections on ingredients and equipment, and basic preparation. It is important to be hygenic, to wash your hands before preparing foods, and use clean utensils. Try also to use natural cleaning products, as they have no, or less-toxic, chemicals.

Vegetables

Organic vegetables are always recommended. It is not good for our health and well-being to eat vegetables and fruit sprayed with toxins. Some non-organic vegetables are worse to eat than others, and these are commonly referred to as the dirty dozen. This list varies slightly from year to year depending on what comes up in testing, but the following are regularly included: strawberries, apples, pears, nectarines, peaches, grapes, cherries, tomatoes, bell peppers, spinach, cucumbers, celery, snap peas and potatoes. It is more expensive to buy but I would suggest you try to go organic on at least these ones.

Specifically, when it comes to fermentation, organic is absolutely best to use. For example, non-organic vegetables sometimes rot rather than ferment. They can turn into mush rather than ferment to the usual crispy consistency. Nonetheless, one of the great benefits of fermenting is that the process helps remove toxins from the vegetables, both natural toxins and added ones like pesticides and herbicides. This means the fermented version of a sprayed vegetable will have fewer toxins than the fresh version of the same sprayed vegetable. So, fermenting your non-organic vegetables is much less toxic than eating them in their non-fermented form. I have fermented plenty of non-organic vegetables and they mostly turn out fine – although organic vegetables always turn out better. Organic fermented vegetables taste better, smell better, and usually have a crisper texture.

Below and opposite: Locally grown organic vegetables are the best choice, but non-organic is much better than no vegetables at all. Source the freshest you can from local farmers wherever possible, but don't worry if supermarket veg is what you have, the ferments will still be good for you.

It also makes a difference if the vegetables you ferment are fresh and in season. The fresher the vegetable is, the more nutritious it is and the more sugar and water it contains – as mentioned earlier, sugar is vital for the fermentation process as this is what gets made into lactic acid. The more natural sugar in the vegetable, the better it will ferment. The breakdown of sugar starts as soon as a vegetable is picked, and the longer it is stored the less sugar it will contain. A freshly picked cabbage will make a crispy delicious sauerkraut whereas using a several months-old cabbage could turn out less crispy and less delicious. Having said that, fermentation is still a great way of taking care of excess old vegetables in your fridge. If you become a dedicated fermenter you never have to waste a vegetable ever again.

You should wash your vegetables even if they are organic. The only time you can get away with not washing them is when you grow them yourself. If your vegetables are organic however, there should be no need to peel them, especially as a lot of the good bacteria sits on the skins. You can remove old or discoloured bits if you want to, but overall you can ferment pretty much everything of a vegetable, from top to tail.

Above: I do recommend getting a water filter if you don't have one already, not only for your ferments but for general health. Even a cheap water filter will do the trick. If you have the funds you can go for a more sophisticated reverse-osmosis filter that is fitted to your sink, or a free-standing filter.

Water

If you use water in your ferments, as in brine fermentation, there are some rules to follow. Firstly, it cannot contain chlorine as this will affect the ferment in a negative way. This means that if you use normal tap or faucet water you need to filter it or boil it before use. Another way, although time-consuming, to get the chlorine out is to leave it to evaporate naturally for 24 hours. Most water filters, including jug filters, will filter out chlorine. If you have your own water well it will probably not be chlorinated and the water can be used without boiling or filtering. Bought still spring water or mineral water can also be used.

Secondly, the temperature of the water used in any fermentation should be of room temperature or finger-warm. If it is too hot then it will kill the bacteria or culture used. If you boil your water you need to wait until it has cooled down to room temperature, no warmer than 35°C or 95°F.

Unless you have your own source of clean spring water I suggest you invest in a quality water filter. This will be a good investment for your ferments but more importantly it will be a good investment for your health. The chemical toxins, heavy metal, bacteria, hormones and even traces of drugs found in some tap water today is nothing anyone should be drinking on a regular basis. Filtering your tap water will get much more toxins out than boiling your tap water.

Salt

My aunt Birgitta, who has over 40 years' experience of making traditional fermented foods, would say that salt is vital for the fermentation process and without it the vegetables might rot instead of ferment. Other experts, including Mr Sandor Ellix Katz, say that salt is not necessary for fermentation. However, the likelihood of a successful ferment is much higher if you do include salt.

Some people have been told by their doctor to reduce their salt intake, for example if they have high blood pressure or severe kidney problems. You should in these cases choose to omit the salt and instead use something like seaweed that has a natural salty taste as well as minerals. If you have high blood pressure or kidney problems you must consult your cardiologist or nephrologist for more advice, if you are unsure about using salt in your ferments.

This might cause the rest of us to question if we should include salt in the ferment or not, and it is true that too much salt can be bad for health. However let's look at this a little bit more closely. Not all, but some, people who are told they need to reduce their salt intake do eat a lot of processed and fabricated foods, which contain enormous amounts of salt. The salt used in processed food is the cheapest on the market and is commonly known as table salt or cooking salt. Table salt is a processed salt that has been stripped of its minerals, often bleached and mixed with various additives, such as sodium ferrocyanide, talc and aluminium, to make it flow better and stop it from clumping together. These low-quality salts can be damaging to your health, and are best excluded from your diet. This salt

REASONS TO INCLUDE SALT IN A FERMENT:

- Salt will add essential minerals to your ferment, making it more nutritious.
- Salt will help with the osmosis, meaning it will draw the water out of the vegetables, which is something we want to happen in dry or non-brine fermentation.
- Salt will increase the preservation of the food – it will stop certain bad bacteria coming into the ferment and it will stop yeast from growing so that the vegetables do not rot or turn into alcohol. It will also prevent mould from growing on top of the ferment.
- Salt will keep the vegetables crisp. If there is no or too little salt, the ferment often goes soft or soggy.
- Salt will enhance the taste of your ferment. A ferment without salt is not very nice-tasting at all in my experience, I would say it is edible but less enjoyable.

If you still do not want to use any salt in your ferment you could choose to use some naturally salty sea vegetables instead or tamari. This will ensure you get some lovely minerals in your ferment and may still help to keep your fermented foods crisp.

might also include added iodine, which is an important mineral but not good to use in your ferment as it is highly anti-bacterial and will interfere with the fermentation process.

Unrefined and unadulterated sea salts and rock salt on the other hand are not harmful in low amounts. Unrefined sea salts and unadulterated rock salts are full of minerals in a bioavailable form, and are the only salts that you should use on your ferments and in any other food preparation for that matter. I like to use Celtic sea salt or pink Himalayan rock salt. It is better to use finely ground salt, as this dissolves more easily. However, a good quality salt should dissolve well anyway, and larger crystals should also be fine to use if that is what you have, even if they are not my first choice. Pickling salt is not recommended; although it has no added iodine it is still a table/cooking salt and therefore not good for our health. Kosher salt is a natural sea salt and can be used, although it is coarse rather than fine.

Salt will increase your chances of creating a good ferment. When you start out you should follow the recommended amount of salt, which is around 1.5% of the ferment in weight in a dry fermentation and 3–5% of however much liquid you are using in a brine fermentation. For example, 1.5% in a dry fermentation using 1kg/2¼lb of vegetables = 15g (½oz) of salt or 1 tablespoon; 3% of salt in a brine fermentation using 1 litre/1¾ pints of water = 30g (1oz) of salt or 2 tablespoons. It is easy to add too much salt in the beginning, so try to follow these recommended amounts.

Salt slows down the fermentation process, which is useful in hot countries and hot weather. If it is very cold when you ferment your vegetables you can use less salt – if it is hot then use a bit more. However, too much salt will have a negative effect on the first phase of fermentation, making the second phase start much sooner than it should. This will make a sharper and more sour ferment. 1.5% salt is ideal but anything between 0.5–3% usually turns out fine. In brine fermentation, up to 5% is fine. Too much salt is not going to taste nice and is bad for our health, though do remember that salt is one of the ways to keep out unwanted bacteria, so less salt means a bigger risk for mould. If you are unsure about using salt, I have included a low-sodium recipe on page 82.

Below: Salt is the magic ingredient in a ferment, protecting it from unwanted bacteria while allowing the good bacteria to grow, helping to retain vegetable crispness and crunch, and adding flavour.

Starters

Type of starter	Approx amount
Probiotic capsule	1 (content of)
Probiotic powder	2.5g/½ tsp
Dairy whey	50ml/1¾fl oz
Water kefir (liquid)	60ml/2fl oz
Kombucha	60ml/2fl oz
Liquid from a previous batch of sauerkraut	50ml/1¾fl oz
Nut whey	50ml/1¾fl oz
Rejuvelac	60ml/2fl oz
Ginger bug	50ml/1¾fl oz
Apple cider vinegar (raw with mother)	50ml/1¾fl oz

The list compares the quantity of 1 probiotic capsule that you would open up and use the powder from. So if the recipe requires 1 probiotic capsule then you can swap it for what is listed above, if you prefer to use that instead. These amounts are approximate, and it can depend on how active a starter is and also what brand of probiotic is used. The starters are vegan except the dairy whey, although if you are vegan check the probiotic capsule or powder as many are derived from dairy.

A starter, in the world of fermentation, means something that will accelerate or enhance the fermentation process. The addition of a starter means that you will 'culture' your ferment rather than 'wild ferment' it. Vegetable ferments don't need a starter or a culture, but some fermenters like to use additional starters. Starter cultures are only needed when fermenting fruit, drinks, grains and dairy, but they are sometimes also used when fermenting vegetables – dairy whey, for instance, is often used as a starter culture in American recipes although you would never see it in European recipes. Other examples of starter are nut whey, the liquid from a previous batch of fermented vegetables, probiotic powder, apple cider vinegar, rejuvelac, ginger bug, and various types of SCOBY (described on page 138).

The theory is that starters will help the ferment to come out better and taste better, as well as controlling the bacteria in the ferment and preventing unwanted bacteria. Personally, I don't much like vegetable ferments with whey, and in this book there are no vegetable ferments with added starters. However, some health authorities suggest it is good to use something to control the ferment, and if you want to add one, probiotic powder will not change the flavour as much as whey.

Some ferments, unlike vegetable ferments, do need a starter or a culture for fermentation to happen. For example kombucha, kefir and sourdough bread would be impossible to make without their specific starter culture.

This book includes recipes with and without starters but I will only suggest using a starter if it is necessary. The recipes that call for a starter mostly require probiotic powder. However, should you want to use something different, the chart to the left lists examples of other starters you can use – you will find details about them later in the book. These can be used in any recipe that requires a starter, apart from milk kefir, yogurt, sourdough bread, water kefir and kombucha. Milk kefir grains are not on the list as they are only used for fermenting dairy kefir, nor kombucha scoby as this is only used for making kombucha. I have included apple cider vinegar but be aware this does not always work as well as the other starters. Remember, fermentation is an art and the same recipe can come out differently from time to time.

Equipment

You don't really need much equipment for fermentation, other than a suitable jar or crock to put the ferment in: your essentials are basically a sharp knife, a chopping board and a mixing bowl, and measuring scales. But there are other items that are useful, and a few things to remember.

A pounder is good when you make big batches, to make sure your vegetables are really tightly packed (when making smaller batches, your fist will do the job fine). You can buy special pounders but there are things in the kitchen already that can work well – a pestle for instance, or a straight-ended rolling pin. And sticky labels are useful for naming and dating your ferments; it's easy to forget when the jars are lined up on the shelf.

You will need a clean muslin or cotton tea cloth for covering some of your ferment jars (with elastic bands or string to tie), and if you are making thick yogurts and cheeses you will need a muslin, cheesecloth or nut-milk bag to drain them in.

The following equipment is not essential but might be of some help. A grater or a peeler is useful if you want to grate your vegetables rather than chop or slice them with a knife. There are also special fermentation graters, which are huge boards that are very quick to grate on. A mandoline can be good, as you can chop and grate to whatever size you want, although in my experience they are quite sharp and have less protection for your fingers, so take care. A food processor is quick and easy and often comes with various attachments that can chop and grate in various sizes.You could even use a spiraliser to slice vegetables! A dehydrator will dry products without having to heat them – I have mentioned it in some of the recipes – it is not something you need when you start fermenting, however if you want to make a lot of nut cheeses then a dehydrator could be useful.

Above and below: A range of simple cutting tools will help slice vegetables to the desired size and length – a sharp cleaver, a mandoline, a grater for finer textures, or of course a food processor which has a variety of grating and chopping blades.

Jars and Crockpots

There are a few things to think about when you choose your container for fermentation. The jars will host your ferment for at least three weeks so they need to be of good quality. Avoid using metal containers as the ferment can corrode the surface of the metal and this can react with the contents in a negative way. Also avoid using plastic, as the acidity of the ferment can leach out chemicals from the plastic even if it is food-grade or BPA-free. You may see some people using plastic to ferment in, and it is practical, but personally I would refrain from doing this in case it leaches chemicals on to your food that are unhealthy to ingest. The best materials to use are ceramic, clay or glass containers. Make sure they are all lead-free; some older crockpots might have lead in the glaze for instance. Also make sure your jar is free of cracks as these can introduce contamination.

The rule about not using metal and plastic applies to the actual fermentation stage. When you are preparing your vegetables, it does not matter what material you use; it is only when the fermentation sits and ferments that you need to be careful. Also, if lids are made from metal or plastic it does not matter as long as they do not touch the ferment directly.

There are also things to consider with the lids. Preferably, do not use a lid that you have to unscrew to get off. There will be a build-up of gases inside

your fermentation jar and if you do not open the lid regularly to let it out, a screw-lid will become impossible to open. The jars I recommend using are the kilner-style glass jars with a rubber seal and clip-on lids. They have a wide opening that makes it easy to add the vegetables, and the lid is simple to open and shut when you need to let the gases out. You might see pictures of vegetables fermenting without a lid, but I would not recommend this as it welcomes little bugs, oxygen and bacteria.

There is a variety of specially-made pots for fermentation, which are described overleaf. These are great as they normally come with weights that will help keep your vegetables submerged beneath water. Most of these jars have an airlock which allows the gases to come out without you having to open it. This means no other bacteria can enter into the ferment. These purpose-made jars are good, but if you don't want to buy one they are not necessary.

It is helpful if the opening of the jar is big enough to fit your fist. This makes it easier to pack and pound the vegetables in properly.

Most recipes require a 1.5-litre/2½-pint jar for fermentation. This is not a strict rule and if you have only smaller jars then just make it in several of them. If you have a 2- or 3-litre jar, make it in that. I suggest using a jar big enough so that it will definitely not over-fill. It is much better to do your ferment in larger quantities in a bigger jar and then to decant into smaller jars for storage. Ferments do turn out better in larger quantities, both in taste and in crispness. It does not matter if your fermentation jar does not get completely filled up with vegetables. In fact it is good to have a gap as gases are formed during the process and will need somewhere to go.

CLEANING JARS

In any food preparation you need to be careful with hygiene. Washing your hands with soap and water is the most effective way not to spread bacteria. The same principles apply when you do your fermentation. You need to wash your hands before food preparation, and you need to wash your jar well with something that will clean it effectively. I suggest using a natural

Right and opposite: You can use most ordinary clean glass jars with a good lid for fermentation, but they will need opening every day, and so the large kilner-style jars with seals and clip-on lids are better for quick and easy opening. Smaller jars with screw-on lids are more suitable for storing your decanted ferments in the fridge.

detergent with no chemicals. Bicarbonate of soda (baking soda) is also a fantastic natural detergent and one that is often suggested by the makers of professional fermentation pots and jars. Vinegar is another natural detergent you can use.

You can wash your jars by hand or in the dishwasher. It is not necessary to sterilise your jars for home fermentation but of course there is no rule that says you can't. For example, you can let your jars sit in boiling-hot water for a while or put them in the oven on 100°C/212°F for 15 minutes. Be aware that glass jars can be sensitive to hot water or high temperatures in the oven, and never put cold food in a hot glass jar or cold water in a hot glass jar, or they will crack. Take care handling hot water and use protective oven mitts. Separate the seals from the jars during cleaning. Check the jars for any damage such as cracks and breaks before using.

Fermentation Lids

You can also get special fermentation lids that will fit your glass jar, instead of a screw-on lid. These are easy to find online and do not cost a lot. This lid enables the gases to get out whilst stopping anything getting in, preventing explosions and unwanted bacteria. All you do is screw them on and you do not have to unscrew or even touch the ferment until it is ready. The lids vary in type but all have a version of one-way airlocks.

You will still need to use weights to ensure the vegetables stay under the liquid during fermentation. In these pictures you can see the use of a stone as a weight – no need to buy any expensive weights when nature will provide you with ones for free! Make sure you boil the stones though for some time to get rid of unwanted bacteria and other microorganisms.

Below: Here I am using a clean jar with a special fermentation lid, and am pressing down the ferments below the surface using the boiled stone trick. These combined measures will help eliminate risk of unwanted bacteria or mould getting into the ferment.

The Fermentation Pot

A fermentation crockpot is a great option. It is large and wide with thick walls; the shape varies but the one shown here is typical. The pot keeps the ferments cool and at the same temperature for the whole process. It is made from clay, so your ferment will be effectively in the dark even though you might put it on your kitchen bench. It comes with specially designed weights that you use to press your ferment underneath the water, which is very convenient. Finally, it has a lid that you do not need to open during the process.This particular crockpot has a water lock, though there are other types available. You fill an outer ridge up with water and then you put the lid down into the water. This way, the gases being made during the fermentation process will be able to come out and yet nothing will be able to get in. This prevents any incoming bacteria and you don't have to remember to burp the jar daily.

Below: Using a special fermention pot is a simple process. Firstly you add your prepared vegetables and pack them in tightly. Then you add the weights and push them down so that the liquid rises above the vegetables. Then you add water into the ridge in the water lock, and finally you put the lid on.

Weights

As you will read later, for a successful ferment vegetables need to be tightly packed underneath water without any air bubbles. This is either under their own naturally produced water or under an added brine. Failure to ensure this liquid coverage is one of the main reasons for an unsuccessful ferment. I meet many people who say their ferments have started to mould or tasted 'off' when trying it. This may well be because the vegetables were not completely submerged in water. Check your ferments are underneath water regularly, adding more liquid if needed. And to help the ferment stay underwater you usually need some sort of weight to push it down.

There are several ways to make sure the vegetables stay tightly packed underneath water. If you are using a professional fermentation crockpot (see previous page), it will come with its own weights that you put on top of your vegetables, pressing them down underneath the water. You can also buy special fermentation weights separately, in various sizes. These options are fine but they cost money and they are not necessary as you can use what you have got at home already. These are the three tricks I usually use.

THE CABBAGE LEAF TRICK

This is my preferred way of pushing down the ferments in the jar, using the natural material that you already have to hand.

Top: Put a leaf of cabbage on top of the vegetables in the clip-top jar.

Above: Now push down the peeled stalk of your cabbage. The stalk should be tall enough to come just above the opening so that the jar lid pushes it down.

Right: Push the lid down tightly to seal. You can also add a sterilised stone or even a small clean glass to push down the vegetables further if you don't have a big enough stalk.

THE PLASTIC BAG TRICK

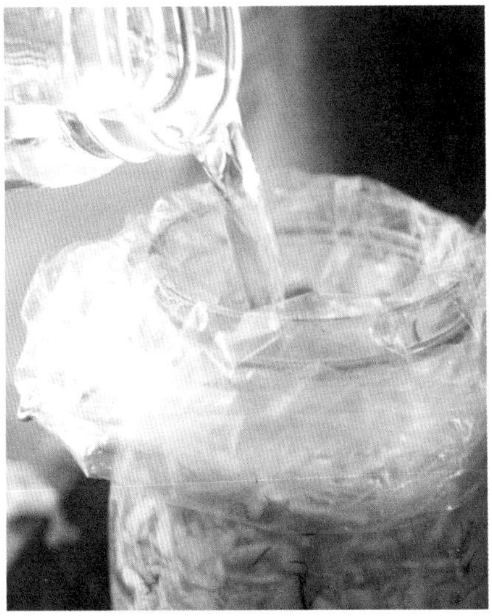

I personally prefer the other tricks, as this one uses plastic, but it is practical. First, put a food-grade plastic bag inside the jar (making sure it is big enough for the jar).

Pour water straight into the bag in-situ, suck out all the air, and then tie the top together. (Zip-up bags don't work for this.)

The air bag is like a cushion on top of your vegetables. If you don't want plastic to touch the ferment you can use a cabbage leaf in between.

THE BOILED STONE TRICK

Using stones as a weight is both cheap and effective. You just need to find a good shape that fits into your jar. First boil the stones to sterilise them.

Put the stones into the jar, adding as many as you need to push the ferment underneath the liquid.

You might need a few stones, depending on the size of the gap.

Storing your Ferment

The temperature where you leave your jars to ferment is important, and should ideally be between 18–20°C/65–68°F. The warmer it is, the quicker something will ferment, and the colder it is, the longer it will take. Ideally a little bit colder is better than too warm, but it is hard to find coolness in many modern houses and kitchens. Commercially, sauerkrauts are fermented at around 20–22°C/68–72°F, then after a day or two the temperature is taken down to 15°C/60°F. To be able to achieve this at home you would need a cold room or a cellar.

However, saying this, when I store my ferments at home in my kitchen the temperature is a little warmer than ideal, around 20–22°C/68–72°F, and I find this works absolutely fine in practice. The lactic acid bacteria are pretty hardy and will survive, even in less favourable temperatures. There is no need to worry too much. Remember as well, the larger the batches, the cooler the ferment will be, and the better they will turn out, so make bigger quantities if you can.

Ideally a ferment is best kept in the dark. A cupboard is good, or you can use a clay pot or even try covering your jar with a towel. However I have fermented many batches left uncovered in glass jars on my kitchen bench, and this normally still works well. So again, there is no need to worry too much if there is no dark place to store your ferments.

When your ferment is ready to eat, it is time to transfer it to the fridge. At this point, when transferring to the fridge, the fermentation process will stop. Of course, fermentations were first made long before the fridge was invented, and they were simply stored in as cold and dark a place as possible. Your fermentations can be stored outside the fridge but be mindful that the fermentation process will still continue to a degree. If you have a cold cellar you can store it there and it will keep almost as well as in the fridge.

If you keep it out on your kitchen bench or on a shelf it should keep for a few months, but not as long as in the fridge. You do also need to be even more careful with hygiene if you store your ferments outside of the fridge. If you have a small fridge and no cold cellar I would suggest you make smaller batches of fermented foods rather than large ones, and just make them more regularly.

I normally ferment in a large pot as larger batches do tend to come out much better than smaller batches. Then, when the ferment is ready, I will transfer it into smaller pots, like jam jars. Ordinary jars and pots with screw lids are now absolutely fine to use. As long as the jars are clean and you don't open them up, these potted ferments will last for several months in the fridge. Perhaps even years! The fermentation process will continue only very slowly in the fridge, although the taste and the texture may intensify with time. Ferments never last that long in my fridge, as they get eaten up very quickly, but I have tried ferments that have been kept for several years and they are still freshly crisp and lovely to taste.

As soon as you open a jar and start spooning out the contents, it will not last that long and it will eventually go off just like any other jarred food. An opened jar is best kept in the fridge and will not keep for several months or years, so you need to be as mindful of hygiene as with other jars of food.

Opposite: While the fermentation process is happening and gases building up, it is very important to regularly burp the jars, and to keep an eye on them; a bursting jar is very rare but has been known to happen. Once the fermentation process is finished, you can store the jars in the fridge or somewhere dark and cold in the cellar, house or garage, although I have often kept them in my light kitchen without a problem. Once they are opened it is best to store them in the fridge.

The Dry-Salt Ferment

This method is used when making normal sauerkraut and most other ferments. It is the most common way to ferment vegetables and is my preferred technique. The ferments come out fresh and crisp in texture and it is the easiest method to succeed with. This type of fermenting suits vegetables that are cut fairly small, grated, thinly sliced or julienned.

1 Preparing the vegetables. Wash them and remove outer damaged or dirty leaves. Don't throw anything away yet, just set it aside as you might find a use for it later as a weight. Root vegetables can be washed or peeled depending on how dirty they are. If they are non-organic, I would always peel them. I usually keep the core or stalk of the cabbage to use later as a weight to push the vegetables down with (see page 38).

2 Chopping the vegetables. Grate, cut or chop the vegetables to the size you would like them. The finer you cut, the easier it is to massage the vegetables later. You can chop the vegetables by hand with a sharp knife or use a vegetable grater, a mandoline, or even a food processor. When I am feeling lazy or making a large batch I use my food processor to chop and grate. How you cut and chop your vegetables is up to you. Just remember if you chop them too big it might be harder to get any water out.

3 Salting the vegetables. The salt will help with the breakdown and the osmosis of water in the vegetables and make the massaging a lot easier. Weigh the vegetables and put them in a bowl, then add the right amount of good-quality salt. As a guide, 1.5% of the weight of the vegetables is a good measurement to remember. This means that to 1kg/2¼lb vegetables, 15g/½oz of salt should be added. Depending on what salt you use, 1 tablespoon of salt is 15–19 ml or grams, so to make it easy just think of the ratio as 1 tbsp of salt to 1kg vegetables. Do not just rely on tasting to judge the ferment salt level, if you are a beginner, as the salty flavour will totally change during the fermentation process.

4 Massaging the vegetables. The fermentation process is initiated when the vegetables start to break down. Massaging or pounding the vegetables will start this and help ensure the fermentation process happens evenly. It also speeds up the chemical process of osmosis, which is the movement of water from within the vegetable. This is the leaked water that eventually covers the vegetables and maintains the anaerobic environment that is needed for a successful fermentation.

Below: I generally thinly slice cabbage or grate it using a mandoline, but for carrots and beet I prefer to julienne them or grate them coarsely on a vegetable grater.

First, mix your veggies together well with your hands using a firm massaging motion. This could take up to 5 minutes depending on the strength of your hands. You could also leave the vegetables to soak in the salt for 15 minutes before you massage them to soften them up and reduce the massaging time. Now is also the point to add any spices and herbs to your ferment if you are using them. Once you start to see juice in the bottom of your bowl and the vegetables start to look more opaque and 'cooked' in consistency you can stop massaging. If your vegetables are fresh and in season this will happen more quickly than if the vegetables are out of season or stored.

Another way of breaking down the vegetables is to pound them lightly. There are special fermentation pounders you can get but you could also use a rolling pin or a meat hammer or similar utensil you might have at home. Again, when the vegetables start to look more wilted and water is starting to come out, you can stop pounding.

If no liquid comes out, there are a number of possible reasons. Perhaps you haven't massaged the vegetables enough, or the vegetable is cut up too large, or if you are using too-old vegetables with not much water. I would suggest you take your time massaging the vegetables or leave them to soak for a while in the salt before massaging, to allow osmosis to begin. If there is still no liquid coming out, the vegetable is probably better suited to a brine fermentation.

5 Packing the vegetables. After pounding or massaging it is time to start packing your vegetables in a clean fermentation jar. Pack the vegetables in tightly, either with your hands or using a pounder or other suitable utensil. I find using my hands or fists will do this the best. Start by putting a quarter of the vegetables in the jar and push down firmly with your fist. Then add another quarter and press down firmly, and so on. Don't put all of the vegetables in the jar at once as there is a risk that pockets of air will form and the ferment go wrong.

Above: I like vegetables to be quite thinly shredded in my dry-salt fermentations.

HERBS AND SPICES:

I also like using herbs in my ferments as much as possible. Not only do they give extra flavour, but herbs and spices are full of nutrients, and they will be even more nutritious when fermented. For example turmeric is anti-inflammatory, anti-cancerous and high in antioxidants. Cinnamon is a good gut healer as well as great for balancing blood sugar. Ginger is anti-inflammatory and also a gut healer. You will have to experiment with how much to add – if you add too much the flavour can be bitter or a little too perfumed. These are the spices and herbs that I find work particularly well: dill, caraway, cumin, mustard seeds, horseradish, raspberry leaves, blackcurrant leaves, juniper berries, tarragon, turmeric, cayenne, cinnamon, rosemary, thyme, savory, bay leaf, and whole pepper. You can use the plant or the seeds, dried or fresh.

Above: You really need to get kneading to instigate the osmosis or movement of water. Massage the vegetables hard until they look slightly cooked or wilted.

The vegetables will expand slightly when they start to ferment, so you do not want to fill the jar all the way to the top. Leave at least a 5cm/2in gap between the vegetables and the opening of the jar. Gases will form during the fermentation process and it needs somewhere to go. If you leave a too-small gap, the liquid from the ferment will start to seep out of the jar and make a mess in your kitchen. If you have a larger gap it does not matter. If you are unsure whether you have left a big enough gap you could put the jar on a plate to catch any potential spills.

6 Weighting the vegetables. When you have finished packing the jar, the liquid should rise above the vegetables. To keep the vegetables underneath the water you might have to press them down using some kind of weight. If you have a proper fermentation jar it often comes with special weights that you can use. Otherwise you can use one of the suggested methods on pages 38–9 to push the vegetables down underneath the water level.

Sometimes there is just not enough water to cover the vegetables. If you have followed the salting and massaging instructions and there is still not enough water, it is fine to add a bit of filtered water to cover the vegetables. Or if you have some salty brine made up you could add this to cover the ferment.

7 Fermenting. So, you have now chopped, salted, massaged and packed the vegetables tightly and there are no air bubbles with oxygen hiding in your ferment. The water from the vegetables is covering them completely. You have put some sort of weight on top so that the vegetables stay under the surface, and tightly secured the lid on the jar. Congratulations, you are now done with most of the work. Now it is all about waiting – which is usually the hardest part.

You need to put this ferment in a place where it is not in the way and where it can stay for 3 weeks or longer. Somewhere in the kitchen out of direct sunlight is good. As discussed earlier the ideal temperature for fermenting is between 18–20°C/65–68°F. If you have a cellar you can move the ferment there after a day or so in the kitchen. Otherwise just keep it in the same place for the duration. I do all my ferments in my kitchen and they generally work fine, and means they are accessible to check on and to release the gases regularly.

8 Burping the jar. During the fermentation process gases will be produced and pressure will build up inside your jar. If you have a proper fermentation jar or a fermentation lid to your mason jar, the gases will be let out without you having to do anything. However, if you are using a kilner-style jar with a clip-on lid and a rubber ring, then you have to burp the jar. Quickly release the lid to let the gases out and then tightly secure the lid again. This is especially important to do in the beginning of the process, but once a day should be enough. Your ferment might burp more or less depending on how large your jar is and how much space you have between your vegetables and jar opening. If you ensure you have a jar with a tight-fitting lid, it will need to burp one way or another.

9 Checking the liquid level. Sometimes the water will evaporate during the fermentation and, in these instances, you could also add a little bit of filtered water. If you do add more than 50ml/1¾fl oz of filtered water

Below: Add a little bit of the vegetables at a time so that you can make sure it is tightly packed in without any air bubbles. The water level needs to be above the vegetables when done. If not then add some filtered water as well.

to your dry ferment, you need to dissolve 1% of salt in it before adding to make a salty brine – that means 1g or ¼ tsp salt to 100ml/3½fl oz water.

10 How long to ferment. If you want all the probiotic benefits it is important to let your vegetables ferment so that both stages of fermentation take place fully. Remember that this take around 3 weeks depending on temperature, salt and a few other variables. Some vegetables ferment slightly quicker than others. The more sugar in the vegetable, the quicker it ferments. Each recipe in this book will give a suggested time for the ferment. However, if it's mainly the taste you are after then you can start eating it as early as 5–7 days. You might prefer the milder taste of a very young ferment or you might prefer the taste of a 6-week mature ferment with its deep flavours; less crunchy but still with a crisp texture. The best way to judge the result is to taste it.

Below: I frequently use a cabbage leaf and then a chunk of peeled cabbage stalk to push down the vegetables underneath the water level in the jar.

11 Checking it's ready. When the fermentation is finished you can carefully take away the weights you have been using as well as any cabbage leaves or similar that have been helping to push the vegetables down. Make sure there is no mould growing on the top; this should not happen if you have been following the instructions well but can occur sometimes if you are using vegetables to push the ferment down with. More commonly you might see a white layer on top. This is yeast and totally harmless although it does not taste good; carefully scrape this off and it will be perfectly fine underneath. If there is mould, however, I suggest you throw the ferment away as mould is not healthy to ingest. The reason for mould is one of three in my experience: the vegetables have not been fermented underneath the water surface; there is too little salt in the ferment; or the jar does not have a sufficiently protective lid. It might also be due to the quality of vegetables, or if the room you ferment in is damp and mouldy.

12 Storing. When your ferment is ready to eat, it is time to transfer it to the fridge. If you are lucky enough to have a cold cellar you can also keep it there. I normally ferment in a large fermentation pot as large batches come out much better than smaller batches. Then, when the ferment is ready, I transfer it into smaller pots. Pots with screw lids are now absolutely fine to use. Pack the fermented vegetables tight into the storage pots; they can be filled up, with no gaps. If you know you are going to keep them for several months you could add a very small amount of extra virgin olive oil to cover the surface only. As long as the pots are well-cleaned and not opened, these ferments will last for several months, possibly even years in the fridge.

The Brine Ferment

If the vegetables you use are cut too large to massage and get any water out of, or if you want to ferment the whole vegetable, or make beautiful patterns in your jar, then brine fermentation is the best method. It is also the better method to use if you want to use less salt in your ferment. Lacto-fermented pickles are done this way. Essentially you just put the vegetables in a jar and pour the made-up salty brine over them to cover completely. No massaging or pounding is needed.

This way of preparing the vegetables is not the same as vinegar pickling. Brine fermentation is made with water and salt. Vinegar pickling (which are conventional commercial pickles) heat-treat the vegetables first to kill the bacteria, then the vegetables are covered with vinegar so that any remaining bacteria will die from the sudden acidity. The undiluted vinegar makes the brine too acidic for fermentation to take place.

Our kind of brine fermenting suits larger pieces of vegetables, whether smaller pickle-size carrots or cucumbers, or whole vegetables like beans and chillies. You can also do this kind of fermentation using sliced, grated and julienned vegetables, although it is more common to dry-ferment these. However, the brine method will work on most types of vegetable.

As for all ferments, it is important to use water that is chlorine-free. This means no tap water. You will need to use water that has been filtered or boiled, or bottled spring or mineral water. Equally important is to use a good-quality salt with no added iodine (see page 30 for more about salt). The amount of salt in a brine fermentation should be between 3–5% of the quantity of water used, not a percentage of the weight of the vegetables as in dry-salt fermentation. So if you are mixing a brine with 1 litre/1¾ pints of water you should use 2–4 tbsp (30–60g/about 1–2oz) of salt. This might sound like a lot of salt but some of it will be taken up by the vegetables,

Below: Add the salt to the water and then stir to dissolve it completely before using the brine. You can warm the water up to make it happen a bit more quickly.

Above: Press down the vegetables firmly in the jar and then add just enough brine to cover them completely. You don't want more liquid than is necessary.

and the water contained in the vegetables will dilute the salty brine. This means that the end result will be the same as found in a dry fermentation, about 1.5%. In summer or hot weather, I would use a bit more salt, 4–5 tbsp (60–75g/about 2–2½oz) as it will help slow down the fermentation in the heat. In winter or cold weather, you can use a little bit less salt, so 2–3 tbsp (30–45g/about 1–1½oz).

You can warm the water up a little bit so that the salt dissolves, however, a good-quality salt should melt in water fairly easily even if it is cold. If you do warm it up then you need to let the solution cool before you use it.

The brine can be flavoured with other spices and herbs as well as salt. Try fresh dill for example, or thyme and bay leaves.

If you make too much brine for your ferment you could keep the excess in the fridge for other ferments you might be making, in case they need a little top-up.

1 Making the brine. This is easy. All you need to do is to add salt to the water and wait until it is dissolved. Nothing else need to be added. Measure your water (filtered or bottled as described above) and stir in the measured salt, then stir to dissolve. If you warm it up to dissolve the salt you need to allow to cool before using. If you make too much brine, you can store it in the fridge until you make your next ferment.

2 Preparing the vegetables. Wash them and remove any outer damaged or dirty leaves or bits. (Don't throw anything away yet; just set it aside for now and you might get a use for it later.) Root vegetables can be washed or peeled depending on how dirty they are. I would suggest peeling them if they are non-organic.

Above: To keep the vegetables below the water surface I normally then use one of my fermentation weights or the boiled stone trick on page 39, before sealing the lid on the jar.

3 Potting (jarring) the vegetables. Make sure the fermentation jar of your choice is washed, cleaned and cooled down. Add your vegetables to the jar. You don't need to pack them tightly, as in dry fermentation, but you still need to press them down using your fist, to minimise the amount of brine needed to cover them. As with dry fermentation, you do not want to fill the jar all the way up to the opening.

4 Adding the brine. Make the brine as described earlier, then pour it over the vegetables, covering them completely. It is very important to always keep the vegetables submerged, but otherwise you don't want excess brine, so keep on pressing the vegetables down well in the jar. The salt in the brine will draw out water from the vegetables so the water content will increase during fermentation. For this reason, as well as to allow space for the gases, make sure there is at least 5cm/2in clear space left in the jar. If this is not practical make sure to put the jar on a plate to catch possible leakage, which can happen if you do not leave a large enough gap.

5 Weighting the ferment. Add a weight to keep the vegetables below the water surface. The tricky part of pickle fermentation is to make sure the vegetables stay below the water surface, at least for the beginning of the fermentation. The vegetables tend to sink down after a few days. If you have a fermentation crockpot this comes with its own weights that are handy to use. You can also buy special fermentation weights. Otherwise I prefer to weight my ferments with boiled stones – see page 39 for details.

6 Fermenting. As with dry-salt ferments, you now need to put this ferment in a place where it is not in the way and where it can stay for 2–3 weeks or longer if you wish. Somewhere in the kitchen out of direct sunlight is good. Again, the ideal temperature is 18–20°C/65-68°F; it is best to have it at this warmer temperature for the first 1 or 2 days and then move it to somewhere colder. Cellars are ideal for storage at the colder temperature but if this is not possible just keep it in a cool place in the kitchen for the duration. As mentioned, you probably don't need to worry too much about measuring ideal temperatures; fermentation will happen anyway and I find keeping the ferments in the kitchen generally works well.

7 Burping the jar. As with dry-salt fermentation, you need to burp your jar unless you are using a special fermentation pot or fermentation lid that makes it possible for gases to come out, and prevent air and bacteria getting inside. Burping just means to open up the lid briefly to let the gases out. Do this once a day, especially at the beginning of the process. You might get away without doing it daily in the later stages when less gas is produced. Depending on the temperature, type of vegetable and size of jar, it can take a day or two before the ferment actually burps, or sometimes it takes only half a day. Don't worry if your ferment doesn't burp much, however; if you have followed the instructions all should be fine.

8 Checking the liquid level. This should not be a problem in brine fermentation, as the liquid will rise rather than get lower. Just make sure the vegetables are submerged under the surface at the beginning.

9 How long to ferment. If you want all the probiotic benefits discussed it is important to let your vegetables ferment so that both stages of fermentation take place fully, just as in dry fermentation. This takes around 3 weeks depending on temperature, salt, and the type of vegetable or fruit. Although brine fermentation seems to be slightly quicker than dry fermentation I would still suggest allowing 2½–3 weeks for most vegetables. Again, this is up to you. You might prefer the taste of a very young ferment or the deeper flavour of a more mature ferment.

10 Storing. When the ferment is ready, transfer it to smaller jars if necessary and put them into the fridge or cold storage. The fermentation process will practically stop in the fridge because of the low temperature. You can store unopened jars of vegetable ferment for months, if not years.

Right: Keep the brined vegetable jar at room temperature for 2–3 weeks to ferment. Remember to burp the jar daily to release the gases. If your jar is full I suggest putting it on a plate to catch any potential liquid spillage.

Vegetable Fermenting Chart

Type of vegetable	Suitability for dry-salt fermentation	Suitability for brine fermentation	Approximate time to ferment in room temperature	Mixes well with other vegetables?
Red cabbage	Yes	Yes	2–3 weeks at least	Great with any vegetable, also apples and spices
White cabbage	Yes	Yes	2–3 weeks at least	Great with any vegetable, also apples and spices
Carrots	Yes	Yes	2 weeks for dry fermentation, 2–3 weeks for brine	Good with white cabbage and spices, but also with most other vegetables if in lesser amounts
Cucumber	Not really but possible	Yes	2 weeks	Best on their own but you could add some carrot, garlic and leaves to keep it crunchy
Tomatoes	Yes as a salsa	Yes	3–5 days with starter for dry fermentation, 2 weeks for brine	Best on their own as these ferment quickly, but can mix with some other vegetables like peppers; good with spices and herbs
Beetroots/beets	Yes	Yes	1–2 weeks for dry fermentation, 2–3 weeks for brine	Good with white and red cabbage, if not so much with other vegetables
Green beans	Not my first choice but possible	Yes	2–3 weeks	Work with most other vegetables
Broccoli	Yes but best with other vegetables	Yes	2–3 weeks	Works with cabbage and most other vegetables
Fennel	Yes	Yes	2–3 weeks	Good with most vegetables
Peppers/bell peppers	Yes when mixed with other vegetables	Yes	2–3 weeks	Good with white cabbage and most other vegetables
Swede	Yes	Yes	2 weeks for dry fermentation, 2–3 weeks for brine	Mixes well with other root vegetables and with cabbage
Parsnip	Yes	Yes	2 weeks for dry fermentation, 2–3 weeks for brine	Mixes well with other root vegetables and with cabbage
Celeriac	Yes	Yes	2 weeks for dry fermentation, 2–3 weeks for brine	Mixes well with other root vegetables and with cabbage
Cauliflower	Yes	Yes	2–3 weeks	Mixes well with most other vegetables
Daikon radish or mooli	Yes	Yes	2–3 weeks	Mixes well with most other vegetables

CHAPTER TWO:

Sauerkrauts

These are the classic dry-salt ferments. This is my favourite way of preparing a ferment. You do have to firmly massage and pack the vegetables, and some people find the method quite hard on the hands, but the result is so delicious it is definitely worth it.

This dry-salt method of fermenting requires you to cut your vegetables fairly thinly or even grate them. The smaller or thinner the vegetable slices, the easier it is to get the water out through osmosis. If you find there is not enough water coming out then just keep massaging a little harder and a little longer. On occasions, especially if you chopped your vegetables too large, you might have to add a bit of filtered water. If you add more water than 100ml per 1kg (3.5fl oz per 2¼lb) of vegetable you might want to add 1% salt to the water to keep the proper percentage of saline.

A traditional sauerkraut is made of cabbage. The best cabbages to use for sauerkraut, in my opinion, are your standard white and red cabbage, especially when fresh and in season. Other types of cabbages are also fine to use of course, although be aware that some (such as Savoy) contain less water than others and it might be that you have to use some additional filtered water or brine. The white and red cabbages are normally tightly packed, firm, and very abundant in water, so you would rarely need to add any liquids to these ferments. I love both red and white cabbage and I use them alternatively, though more often than not I mix them together to create a beautiful pink kraut.

The red cabbage has much more antioxidants so would be slightly healthier. However, tests have shown that fermentation of red cabbage deplete some of the antioxidants so it might not be specially healthier in the end than the white cabbage. Both are good for you!

Cabbage is part of the brassica or cruciferous family which offer highly bioavailable nutrients. Brassicas are true superfoods to include in your daily diet – they are anti-inflammatory, anti-cancerous, fantastic for the liver, and a great source of vitamin C, folic acid and minerals such as iron, selenium, and potassium. There are many health benefits to be had from including cabbage and other brassicas in your diet, and you should include some of these vegetables on a daily basis for good health and longevity. Having some sauerkraut with your lunch or dinner every day is an easy way to get your daily portion of brassica.

Cabbage is good by itself (as pictured opposite) but mixes very well with other vegetables. The greater the variety of vegetables you use, the bigger the range of different kinds of healthy bacteria there will be. Combine cabbage with carrots, beetroots, fennel or celery, for example. Herbs will add other nutritional properties. Pretty much any vegetable can be fermented with this dry-salt method. Be creative and use the following recipes as a guide.

Aunt Birgitta's Sauerkraut

Sauerkraut is called surkal in Swedish. There is no English word for sauerkraut but it literally translates as sour cabbage.

This recipe is a typical Swedish surkal, and a favourite in our household. It can be made with just white cabbage or just red cabbage but personally I prefer a mixture of them both. It will aid your digestion when eaten with a meal and goes well with most dishes. It is good mixed into salads and in coleslaws. If you find sauerkraut a little too sour or sharp for your liking, you can mix in some mayonnaise. This will mellow the kraut and is a great way of giving it to children.

A lovely condiment, this sauerkraut is very versatile. I always come back to this simple recipe.

1.5-LITRE/2½-PINT JAR

500g/1lb white cabbage
500g/1lb red cabbage
2 large apples
15g/1 tbsp good-quality salt
30–60g/2–4 tbsp caraway seeds

1 Wash the cabbages or remove the outer leaves if they are damaged or ugly looking. One medium cabbage weighs around 1kg/2¼lb so if you mix the colours you will need half a cabbage of each.
2 Now grate the cabbages on a mandoline, a hand grater or in the food processor on the slice blade, or cut finely with a sharp knife. The end result should be long thin slices. Grate the apple on a standard coarse vegetable grater. I don't normally use the core of the cabbage, but there is no reason not to. I more often use it as a weight to push down the cabbage in the jar.
3 Put the shredded cabbage and grated apple in a mixing bowl and add the salt and caraway seeds, mixing with your hands. To save your hands, you can leave the bowl standing for 15 minutes for water to come out of the vegetables naturally before massaging.
4 Massage the cabbage until there is a fair amount of water in the bottom of the bowl and the cabbage looks slightly 'cooked'.
5 Transfer the cabbage to your clean fermentation jar, packing it in tightly with your fist or a pounder so that the cabbage is underneath the water surface with no hidden air bubbles. If there is not enough water to cover the vegetables add some filtered water. Leave around 5cm/2in from the surface of water to the lid of the jar. This is to leave enough space for the gases to come out.
6 Put a weight on the vegetables to keep them under the water surface using one of the suggested ways on pages 38–9.
7 Let the vegetables ferment at room temperature for approximately 3 weeks. Check regularly that the vegetables are underneath the water. If you do not use a proper fermentation crockpot or special fermentation lid, don't forget to burp the jar once a day to let the gases out; this means to quickly open the lid to let the air out and then close it.
8 When the ferment is ready, transfer to smaller jars and store in the fridge. It will keep for months if unopened.

For more guidance see the dry-salt ferment instructions on page 44.

Swedish Summer Kraut

I made this sauerkraut for my sister's wedding. They had a buffet-style dinner and wanted to serve locally produced food. It was a late August celebration, and white cabbage is growing everywhere in Sweden at this time so it was an obvious choice of vegetable to ferment, together with freshly picked carrots, red bell pepper and the fresh herbs all flourishing in my mother's garden. I prefer to have the dill stalks in fairly big pieces as it looks nicer. Dill crowns might be tricky to find if you are not growing them yourself, but though normal dill will not give the exact same flavour it will still be very nice. And, if you cannot find the fresh herbs, use dried.

This sauerkraut looks beautiful with the carrots and peppers breaking up the white of the cabbage. It goes well with most dishes – have a tablespoon or two with your meal to aid digestion. It is great stirred into salads and in coleslaws, and lovely mixed with boiled potatoes.

1.5-LITRE/2½-PINT JAR

1kg/2¼lb white cabbage

4 medium carrots

1 red or green bell pepper

small handful of fresh dill stalks including the crowns, torn into pieces

15g/1 tbsp dried juniper berries

15g/1 tbsp caraway seeds

15g/1 tbsp good-quality salt

1 Wash the cabbage and take away the outer leaves if they are damaged or ugly looking. Wash the carrots thoroughly and if they are very dirty or old, peel them. Wash the pepper.

2 Grate the cabbage on a mandoline, a hand grater, or in the food processor on the slice blade, or cut it finely with a sharp knife. The result should be long thin slices. Julienne the carrots in a mandoline or in your food processor. Julienne the pepper with a sharp knife by hand.

3 Put all the vegetables in a mixing bowl and add the herbs, spices and salt, mixing everything together with your hands. Leave for 15 minutes or so for osmosis – the water leakage – to take place.

4 Now do the massaging and as soon as there is enough water in the bottom of the bowl and the vegetables look slightly 'cooked' it is ready for packing. If you use fresh cabbage you will notice a lot of water very quickly.

5 Now pack the massaged vegetables tightly in the clean fermentation jar so that they are underneath the water surface with no air bubbles. When packed leave 5cm/2in between the surface of the water and the lid of the jar for the gases to have space to come out.

6 Put a weight on the vegetables to keep them under the water surface using one of the ways on pages 38–9.

7 Leave the jar to ferment at room temperature for 2–3 weeks. Check regularly that the cabbage is underneath the water surface. If you don't use a proper fermentation pot you will need to burp the jar once a day to let the gases out.

8 When ready, transfer to smaller jars if necessary and store in the fridge. It will keep for months if unopened.

For more guidance see the dry-salt ferment instructions on page 44.

Fresh Turmeric Kraut

This is a lovely-tasting kraut but can turn out a little bitter because of the fresh turmeric. I love the bitterness as it is only slight but if you don't like bitter, use half of the turmeric. Remember that turmeric is a true super-herb and has powerful anti-inflammatory and anti-oxidant properties so it is a good ingredient to eat regularly if not every day. Turmeric may even help delay ageing and to combat age-related chronic diseases, help with depression, and lower the risk of heart disease, and improve brain function and our immune system. We could all do with some of those properties.

I use white cabbage in this recipe as I love the yellow colour the turmeric gives the kraut. This sauerkraut goes well with most dishes and is great with curry dishes, salads and in coleslaws. Have a tablespoon or two with your meal to aid digestion.

Tip: Be aware that the turmeric can stain your hands as well as the utensils that you are using. Wear kitchen gloves if you don't want yellow hands.

1.5-LITRE/2½-PINT JAR

1kg/2¼lb white cabbage
4 medium carrots
2 small pieces of fresh turmeric (3cm/1¼in each)
15g/1 tbsp good-quality salt
10g/2 tsp cumin seeds

1 Wash the cabbage or take away the first few leaves if they are damaged or ugly looking. Wash the carrots thoroughly and peel them if they are very dirty or old. Wash the turmeric and if you prefer, peel it.
2 Grate the cabbage on a mandoline, a hand grater, or in the food processor on the slice blade, or cut it finely with a sharp knife. The result should be long thin slices. Grate the carrots on the coarse blade or julienne if you prefer. Grate the fresh turmeric with the finest blade.
3 Put all the vegetables and turmeric in a mixing bowl, add the salt and cumin, and mix – wear gloves if you want to avoid yellow hands, or use something to stir and to massage or pound the vegetables with. Leave for 15 minutes for the osmosis to happen.
4 Do the massaging or pounding until there is enough water in the bottom of the bowl and the cabbage looks slightly 'cooked'. If you use fresh cabbage you will notice a lot of water very quickly.
5 Now, pack the vegetables tightly in the clean fermentation jar so that the mixed kraut is underneath the water surface with no air bubbles. When packed, leave at least 5cm/2in space from the surface of water to the lid of the jar for the gases to have space to come out.
6 Put a weight on the vegetables to keep them under the water surface using one of the suggested ways on pages 38–9.
7 Leave to ferment at room temperature for 2–3 weeks. Check regularly so that the vegetables are underneath the water surface. If you do not use a proper fermentation crockpot don't forget to burp the jar once a day to let the gases out.
8 When done, transfer to smaller jars if necessary and store in the fridge. The jars will store for months if unopened.

For more guidance see the dry-salt ferment instructions on page 44.

Carrot, Ginger and Cumin Kraut

This is one of my favourite krauts. It is sweet, a little spicy and juicy. For a spicier flavour, you can use more ginger, and of course for a milder version just use a little less. It's not at all the same if you use dried ginger, however, so try and get hold of fresh for this recipe. Root vegetables ferment a little bit quicker than cabbage-based krauts and the warmer it is the quicker it will ferment. This recipe usually takes between 1 and 2 weeks to ferment.

Root krauts are sweet and this goes nicely with most dishes especially curries and Moroccan food. For improved digestion have a couple of tablespoons with your meals. I sometimes add some chopped almonds to this fermented kraut before serving, for a more Moroccan taste. I also often add some grated fresh carrots to freshen up the flavour, and to make a great carrot salad.

1-LITRE/1¾-PINT JAR

1kg/2¼lb carrots
4cm/1½in piece of fresh ginger
15g/1 tbsp cumin seeds
15g/1 tbsp good-quality salt

1 Wash the carrots and ginger. You can peel them or not but if they are clean and organic I suggest keeping the peel on. Cut away any bad bits.
2 Grate the carrot and ginger coarsely either by hand or in a food processor.
3 Put it all in a bowl together with the cumin seeds, add the salt and mix. Leave for 15 minutes if you wish for osmosis to happen first to save your hands, or go straight to the massaging.
4 Do the massaging or pounding and as soon as there is enough water in the bottom of the bowl and the carrots looks slightly 'cooked', it is done. If the carrots are fresh you will end up with enough water. If the carrots are older you might have to add some filtered water.
5 Pack the grated and pounded carrot tightly into the clean fermentation jar so that it is all underneath the water surface with no air bubbles. If there is not enough water to cover, you need to add some. If you are adding more than 50ml/1¾fl oz you need to make a salty brine by dissolving 1% salt in water – that means 1g or ¼ tsp salt to 100ml/3½fl oz water. Leave at least 5cm/2in space from the water surface to the lid of the jar for the gases to come out.
6 Put a weight on the carrots to keep them under the water surface using one of the suggested ways on pages 38–9.
7 Leave the jar to ferment for 1–2 weeks. Check regularly that the carrots are still underneath the water surface. If you do not use a proper fermentation crockpot don't forget to burp the jar once a day to let the built-up gases out.
8 When ready, transfer to smaller jars if necessary and store in the fridge. It will store for months if unopened.

For more guidance see the dry-salt ferment instructions on page 44.

Mixed Root Kraut

This is a sweet-tasting kraut and a perfect way to use your root vegetables. Many people, including myself, do not use enough of these in their cooking even though they are so common in northern Europe. Root vegetables are an amazingly nourishing food that are wonderful to include in your diet, especially in the winter when we all need more warmth and sweetness in our lives. Have this with vegetarian, fish and meat dishes alike. It is a brilliant kraut to add to soups, stews and casseroles.

1-LITRE/1¾-PINT JAR

250g/9oz carrots
250g/9oz swede
250g/9oz celeriac
250g/9oz parsnips
15g/1 tbsp good-quality salt

1 Wash the vegetables thoroughly and peel or cut away any damaged bits. Celeriac for example can be hard to wash all the dirt away so might have to be peeled and cut. You can peel the other vegetables or not, but if they are clean and organic I would keep the peel on, and just cut away any bad bits.
2 Grate the roots coarsely either by hand or with a food processor. Put all into a bowl, add the salt and mix. Leave for 15 minutes for the osmosis (the movement of water out of the vegetable) to happen.
3 Do the massaging or pounding and as soon as there is enough water in the bottom of the bowl and the roots look slightly 'cooked' it is done. If the roots are fresh you will end up with enough water. Otherwise root vegetables tend to lose water quickly if stored for a longer period, and you might need to add a little filtered water.
4 Now pack it tightly into the clean fermentation jar so that the grated roots are underneath the water surface with no air bubbles. If there is not enough water you need to add some. If you need to add more than 50ml/1¾fl oz you should make a salty brine by dissolving 1% salt in water – that means 1g or ¼ tsp salt to 100ml/3½fl oz water. When the vegetables are packed there should be 5cm/2in space from the water surface to the lid of the jar for the gases to come out.
5 Put a weight on the root kraut to keep it under the water surface using one of the suggested ways on pages 38–9.
6 Leave the jar to ferment for 2 weeks. Check regularly that the roots are underneath the water. If you do not use a proper fermentation crockpot don't forget to burp the jar once a day to let the gases out.
7 When done, transfer to smaller jars if necessary and store in the fridge. The kraut will keep for several months unopened.

For more guidance see the dry-salt ferment instructions on page 44.

Sweet Beetroot Kraut

Beetroot has many amazing health benefits. It is said to strengthen and increase resilience. It contains iron, magnesium, folate, betaine and nitrates. It is a great blood cleanser and is a very effective natural remedy for lowering high blood pressure. Studies also show that the increased blood flow caused by eating beetroot will help blood flow to your brain and it may be helpful in the prevention of Alzheimer's and other forms of dementia. It is also a great antioxidant. If you like beetroot you will absolutely love this wonderfully tasty fermentation.

Beetroots are sweet and ferment quickly. I don't usually mix beetroots with anything else as on their own they create a liquid that is sweet and beautifully aromatic and tasty. However, when using only beetroots, the ferment doesn't keep for very long. To increase the preservation, you can mix it with a little bit of cabbage and perhaps onion. Apart from cabbage (see the recipe overleaf), beetroot doesn't go well with other vegetables. It is best to do smaller batches of this as it doesn't keep.

Beetroot kraut is delicious with a salad, and I love it with cheese. Adding some crème fraîche takes it to another level.

1-LITRE/1¾-PINT JAR

500g/1lb beetroots
7.5g/1½ tsp good-quality salt

1 Wash and peel the beetroots, and cut away any bad bits.
2 Julienne the beets thinly on a mandoline or in your food processor.
3 Put the beets in a mixing bowl, add the salt and mix. Leave for 15 minutes to let the water start to come out of the beets.
4 Next, massage or pound the beets, and as soon as there is enough water in the bottom of the bowl and the beets look slightly 'cooked' it is done. Beets as well as other root vegetables create a lot of water if they are fresh; if they have been stored it can be harder to get enough water from them to cover them in the jar. Use gloves for this section unless you want purple hands for the rest of the day!
5 Now pack the beets tightly in the clean fermentation jar so that they are underneath the water surface with no air bubbles. If there is not enough liquid you need to add some filtered water. When packed, leave at least 5cm/2in from the water surface to the lid of the jar for the gases to have space to come out and the beets to expand.
6 Put a weight on the beets to keep them under the water surface using one of the suggested ways on pages 38–9.
7 Leave the jar to ferment at room temperature for around 1–2 weeks. Beets ferment very quickly so if it is warm it might take even less. Smaller batches tend to ferment quicker than larger ones, so check regularly and taste. Also make sure regularly the beets are underneath the water surface. If you do not use a proper fermentation crockpot don't forget to burp the jar once a day to let the gases out.
8 When it is done, move the beet kraut to the fridge. If unopened it will keep several weeks, or longer, but once you open it, eat up quickly.

For more guidance see the dry-salt ferment instructions on page 44.

Beetroot and Cabbage Kraut

If you want your beetroot kraut to last a bit longer you can mix it with cabbage. I usually use white cabbage for this. The kraut will come out differently in taste and texture to the plain beet kraut. It is still very delicious though.

1.5-LITRE/2½-PINT JAR

500g/1lb beetroots
500g/1lb white cabbage
15g/1 tbsp good-quality salt

1 Wash and peel the beetroots, and cut away any bad bits. Prepare the cabbage, taking away the outer leaf and anything that looks bad.
2 Julienne the beets thinly on a mandoline or in your food processor. Do the same with the cabbage – aim for long thin slices of a similar size to the beetroot.
3 Put the beets and cabbage in a mixing bowl, add the salt and mix. Leave for 15 minutes to let the water start to come out of the beets.
4 Next, massage or lightly pound the vegetables, and as soon as there is enough water in the bottom of the bowl and the beets look slightly 'cooked' it is done. Again, if the vegetables are fresh there will be a lot of water coming out but if they have been stored for a while then less water will come out. Use gloves for this stage unless you want purple hands!
5 Now pack the vegetables tightly in the clean fermentation jar so that they are underneath the water surface with no air bubbles. If there is not enough liquid you may need to add some filtered water. When packed, leave at least 5cm/2in from the water surface to the lid of the jar for the gases to have space to come out and the beets to expand.
6 Put a weight on the kraut to keep it under the water surface using one of the suggested ways on pages 38–9.
7 Leave the jar to ferment at room temperature for around 2–3 weeks. It takes slightly longer when the beets are mixed with cabbage. Check regularly that the vegetables are underneath the water surface. If you do not use a proper fermentation crockpot don't forget to burp the jar once a day to let the gases out.
8 When it is done, transfer the kraut to smaller jars if necessary and put them in the fridge. If unopened it will keep several months – much longer than when made with just beets.

For more guidance see the dry-salt ferment instructions on page 44.

Fennel, Chilli and Celery Kraut

I love fermented fennel. It is best to use fennel when it is fresh and in season. The mooli or daikon radish is high in prebiotics which makes this especially good for your digestive health. The recipe is not particularly spicy so if you want a more intense heat, add some more chilli. You can also experiment with different herbs or spices if you wish. This kraut is great with any dish as a digestive aid. Add it to salads and also in cooking for additional flavour.

The recipes uses the fennel bulb, herb and seeds. I grow the leafy herb in my herb garden but if you have trouble finding it, use either dried fennel herb or a few fresh fronds from the bulb.

1.5-LITRE/2½-PINT JAR

800g/1¾lb fresh fennel bulbs

200g/7oz celery

100g/3½oz mooli or daikon radish

15g/1 tbsp good-quality salt

10g/2 tsp fennel seeds

few stalks of fresh fennel herb, torn into smaller pieces

1–2 stalks of fresh thyme, torn into smaller pieces

5–10g/1–2 tsp dried chilli pieces, crumbled, or 10g/2 tsp of chopped fresh chilli

1 Wash the vegetables and cut away any bad bits.
2 Slice both the fennel bulbs and celery thinly on a mandoline or in your food processor with the smallest slice blade added. Grate the mooli.
3 Put the sliced and grated vegetables in a mixing bowl together with the salt, fennel seeds, fennel and thyme stalks, and chilli, and mix with your hands. Leave for 15 minutes so osmosis can take place.
4 Start massaging or lightly pounding the vegetables, and as soon as there is enough water in the bottom of the bowl and they look slightly 'cooked', it is done.
5 Now pack the vegetables tightly in the clean fermentation jar so that they are underneath the water surface with no air bubbles. If there is not enough water you need to add some. If you are adding more than 50ml/1¾fl oz you need to make a salty brine by dissolving 1% salt in water – that means 1g or ¼ tsp salt to 100ml/3½fl oz water. Leave at least 5cm/2in space from the water surface to the lid of the jar for the gases to come out.
6 Put a weight on the vegetables to keep them under the water surface using one of the suggested ways on pages 38–9.
7 Leave the jar to ferment for 2–3 weeks. Check regularly so that the vegetables are underneath the water surface. If you do not use a proper fermentation crockpot don't forget to burp the jar once a day to let the gases out.
8 When done, transfer to smaller jars if necessary and store in the fridge. This kraut will keep for a few months if unopened.

For more guidance see the dry-salt ferment instructions on page 44.

Curried Cauliflower Kraut

Curries are a staple in our house. We love experimenting with Indian spices and recipes. A lot of Indian foods are traditionally fermented, such as dosa, dhokla and rabdi. In Indian cuisine it is mostly cereals, rice and beans that are fermented rather than vegetables. However, Indian spices do work beautifully in vegetable ferments. This curried cauliflower kraut goes well with any curry or other Indian dish.

1.5-LITRE/2½-PINT JAR

800g/1¾lb cauliflower

200g/7oz white cabbage

15g/1 tbsp good-quality salt

15g/1 tbsp freshly grated ginger

10g/2 tsp good-quality curry powder (garam masala is my favourite)

5g/1 tsp cayenne pepper

5g/1 tsp turmeric (fresh chopped or dried ground)

5g/1 tsp cumin seeds

2.5g/½ tsp coriander or nigella seeds

1 Wash the vegetables, removing outer leaves of the cauliflower and cabbage, and cutting away any bad bits.
2 Cut up in small pieces and pulse in a food processor until all are the same size. Do not overdo. I have a Thermomix myself and I process the vegetables together on speed 4 for just 10 seconds. You could also cut finely by hand of course.
3 Put the processed vegetables in a bowl together with the salt and all the spices and mix them with your hands. Leave for 15 minutes for the water to come out.
4 Now massage or lightly pound the vegetables if needed; as soon as there is enough water in the bottom of the bowl and the vegetables look slightly 'cooked' it is done. This should happen fairly quickly as the vegetables are in small pieces.
5 Pack the vegetables tightly in the clean fermentation jar so that they are underneath the water surface with no air bubbles. If there is not enough water you need to add some. If you are adding more than 50ml/1¾fl oz you need to make a salty brine by dissolving 1% salt in filtered water – that means 1g or ¼ tsp salt to 100ml/3½fl oz water. Leave at least 5cm/2in space from the water surface to the lid of the jar for the gases to come out.
6 Put a weight on the vegetables to keep them under the water surface using one of the suggested ways on pages 38–9.
7 Leave the jar to ferment at room temperature for 2–3 weeks. Check regularly so that the vegetables are underneath the water surface. If you do not use a proper fermentation crockpot don't forget to burp the jar once a day to let the gases out.
8 When done, transfer to smaller jars if necessary and store in the fridge where it will keep for several months if unopened.

For more guidance see the dry-salt ferment instructions on page 44.

70 mm

CHAPTER THREE:

Brine Ferments

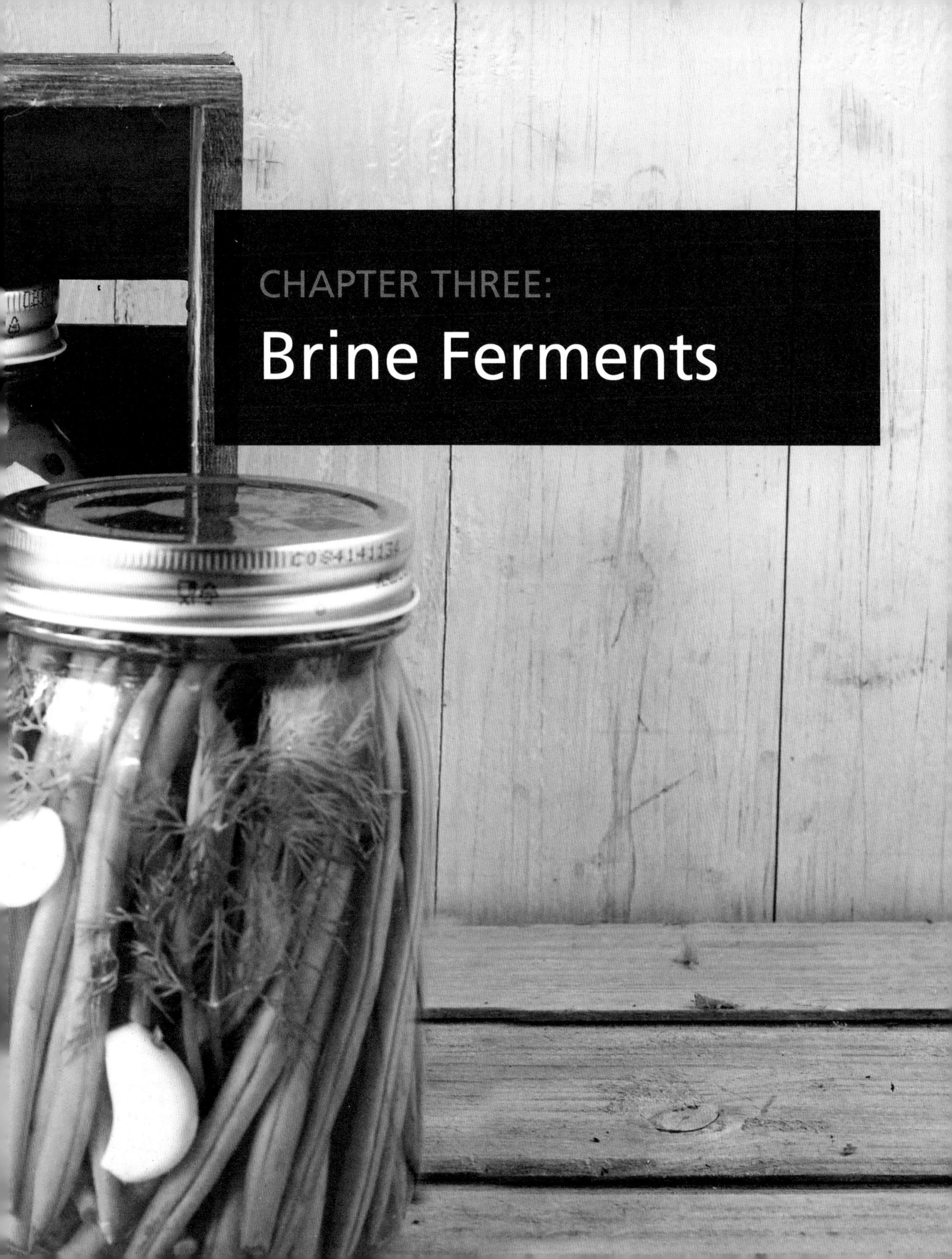

Next up are the brine ferments. Brine-fermented pickles should not be confused with the traditional pickles found in the aisles of supermarkets. These commercial pickles are made with vinegar and sugar, and by pouring boiling water over the vegetables and in that way killing most of the good bacteria. When the vegetables are then put into the vinegar the rest of the bacteria are killed so there is no fermentation going on. Any pickled vegetables you find on a shelf in a supermarket and not in a fridge are all pickled with vinegar and contain no healthy bacteria. In contrast our brine-fermented pickles are made with water and salt only, and contain all the amazing health benefits talked about earlier. Brine fermentation suits large pieces of vegetables that you cannot get the water out of very easily by massaging or pounding. It is also suitable if you want to ferment the vegetables whole or cut into specific shapes. This also means you can create amazing patterns in your jar with careful positioning of the various ingredients.

This method is preferred by many fermenters as it is not necessary to massage or pack down your vegetables. You just pour salty water over them. I personally prefer the taste and texture of the dry-salt ferment method but it is nice how easy and quick this way of fermenting is. I have also often done 'half and half' when there is not enough water coming out through osmosis, meaning I will add some salty brine to my dry-salt ferments where there is not enough water to cover the vegetables. You often need to be creative when fermenting as things might not go exactly to plan.

I sometimes make too much brine for my ferments when using this method. You could either choose to throw the excess brine away but if you are like me, you might like to find a use for it. You could just do another ferment using up old vegetables that might otherwise be thrown away, or store it in the fridge ready for the next ferment. You can even use it in your bath water – salt is both healing for the skin and helpful in drawing out any toxins.

Low-Salt Sauerkraut

This recipe is called a sauerkraut but it is in the brine ferments chapter because it is somewhere between the two. It uses much less salt than other sauerkrauts and therefore it also uses a starter, to speed up the fermentation process and to control the ferment. This sauerkraut is therefore a cultured sauerkraut rather than wild-fermented. As a starter I use probiotic powder but you could use any of the starters on page 32, with the exception of the apple cider vinegar which will not work well. You can also choose a specific strain of probiotic powder if you have a particular digestive problem. For example, Saccharomyces boulardii is good to get rid of Candida as well as Small Intestinal Bacterial Overgrowth (SIBO). Lactobacillus plantarum is good for leaky gut and gut dysbiosis (unbalanced gut microbiome). If you are not sure, any quality probiotic will be good.

I like to use several kinds of vegetables in this ferment, to get the benefits of as many good bacteria as possible. I also add one or two vegetables that are particularly high in prebiotics, such as daikon radish or normal radish. Kale has been hailed as one of the most nutritious vegetables, so fermenting it will make it even more of a superfood. However if you don't like a particular vegetable in this ferment then you can swap for something else like beetroot and celeriac or indeed any other vegetable that you have in your fridge. This method of fermentation is a great way of using up vegetables that are beginning to get old. I don't like food waste so I often do this ferment as soon as I get a build-up of unused vegetables.

This low-salt recipe is slightly different to a normal brine, where you only use water and salt, as I have added a few other things – making it more like a smoothie than a brine in consistency. You can use this smoothie-brine in other ferments as well if you like.

1.5-LITRE/2½-PINT JAR

500g/1lb cabbage
200g/7oz mooli or daikon radish
100g/3½oz carrots
100g/3½oz celery
100g/3½oz kale
10g/2 tsp fresh or dried herbs such as grated fresh turmeric, chopped dill, chopped chives, caraway seeds, or mustard seeds
2 apples
600ml/1 pint filtered or mineral water
5–10g/1–2 tsp good-quality salt or sea vegetables
1–2 probiotic capsules (content only)

1 Wash your vegetables if they are dirty and remove the outer leaves of the cabbage. Set aside the apples to prepare later.
2 Cut the cabbage, mooli, carrots and celery into smaller pieces so that they will fit into your food processor. Depending on what kind of food processor you have, use either the S-blade and pulse the vegetables until they are cut very fine, or use the grating blade and push the vegetables through the shoot. If you don't have a food processor you will have to grate all the vegetables finely by hand. Kale can't be grated, so cut it finely with a knife.
3 Put the shredded vegetables in a mixing bowl, add the fresh or dry spices or herbs, and mix together with your hands. Core and cut up the apples.
4 Now you need to create a brine by mixing the water and the salt. Add the brine and the cut-up apples to a blender and blend until smooth. There should be no bits of apples floating about. You can also add a handful of your shredded vegetables and blend again to a smoothie consistency. Lastly add the probiotic powder from the capsule and stir into the smoothie.
5 Pour the smoothie brine over the shredded vegetables and mix it all together. It should be fairly wet in consistency.

6 Now, transfer the vegetable mix to your clean fermentation jar. Make sure it is tightly packed. It doesn't have to be as tightly packed as a dry-fermented sauerkraut, but you don't want any air bubbles. Leave around 5cm/2in from the surface of water to the lid of the jar, to allow enough space for the gases to come out.

7 You might want to put a weight on the vegetables to keep them under the water surface using one of the suggested ways described on pages 38–9. However, often you don't really need to.

8 Let the vegetables ferment at room temparature for 1–2 weeks. Yes, this kraut is ready sooner than the other recipes, because of the probiotic starter and the low amount of salt, which makes it ferment more quickly. You can ferment it for longer if you wish, however, that is not a problem at all and will only add more good bacteria.

9 Unless you use a proper fermentation crockpot or have a specially designed fermentation lid then don't forget to burp the jar once a day to let the gases out.

10 Store in the fridge when ready. This ferment will last a long time in the fridge if not opened, at least 3–5 months but most probably longer. Be aware though that if you use less salt it won't keep quite so long.

Cauliflower, Carrot and Onion Pickles

This recipe tastes very much like traditional pickles but with the added health benefit of fermentation. Children usually like this as it is mild and sweet. Make sure to use as little salt as possible with young children and infants should have no added salt at all. However, in a brine ferment too little salt will make the vegetables go soft rather than crisp. This pickle is great to serve with any dish and of course as pickles on a mezze board or cheese board. Unless I am making this ferment for children I often like to add herbs and chillies for extra heat and flavour.

1.5-LITRE/2½-PINT JAR

400g/14oz cauliflower
400g/14oz carrots
200g/7oz onions
30–60g/2–4 tbsp good-quality salt
1 litre/1¾ pints filtered water

1 Make the brine by dissolving the salt in the water. You might have to warm the water up a little to do this. Let it cool down before use.
2 Wash the vegetables and cut away any bad bits, the ends of the carrots and the outer peel of the onion.
3 Slice the carrots into 1cm/½in thick coins. Divide the cauliflower into small florets. Cut the onions lengthwise, into quarters, then halve those.
4 Put the vegetables into the clean fermentation jar, pressing them down as hard as possible without damaging them.
5 Now pour the cooled-down brine over the vegetables, covering them completely but with no excess water. You will probably not need all the brine water you have made up, but you could save it and keep it in the fridge if you wish for using in your next fermentation.
6 Put on a weight that keeps the vegetables underneath the water. If you don't have a proper fermentation jar with weights I suggest using the boiled stone or water-filled bag trick on page 39.
7 Leave the jar to ferment for 2–3 weeks at room temperature; I just keep it in my kitchen. Put the jar on a plate as pickles tend to leak out a little, especially if your jar is fairly full. If you do not use a proper fermentation crockpot don't forget to burp the jar once a day to let the gases out.
8 When done, transfer to smaller jars if necessary and store in the fridge. If unopened they will keep for several months.

For more guidance see the brine ferment instructions on page 49.

Fermented Swedish Cucumber

Fermenting cucumbers can be a challenge. This is because they are very watery and their pectin gets broken down very quickly, often leaving them mushy. The best cucumbers to use are small English hothouse cucumbers or Kirby cucumbers. Kirby cucumbers are usually small so you can pickle them whole, which prevents them from going mushy. Another way of preventing them from getting too soft is to add something high in tannin that will reinforce the pectin in the cucumbers. This can be done by adding oak leaves, blackcurrant leaves or grape leaves. More salt will also help, as well as adding some sliced carrots or horseradish. All traditional tricks, discovered over the years. If you can't find the types of cucumbers suggested then try the cucumbers you can find, and see how they turn out.

Something that occurs now and then on my fermented cucumbers is top yeast. This is a white milky covering on top of your ferment and sometimes at the bottom of the jar. It is not dangerous but doesn't taste nice and it means your ferment will not keep for long, so eat it up quickly. The reason for top yeast can be too little salt or too warm a fermentation temperature, which can happen during the summer.

This recipe is a classic and will absolutely become one of your favourite ferments. It is so versatile and can be eaten with almost anything. In Sweden, it is a traditional accompaniment with meatballs and summer herring. I love it on a piece of sourdough toast with nut cheese, avocado and salad.

2-LITRE/3½-PINT JAR

1kg/2¼lb small cucumbers (English or Kirby)
1 carrot
piece of fresh horseradish
4 fresh dill crowns or dill sprigs
6 oak, grape or blackcurrant leaves
10g/2 tsp mustard seeds
5g/1 tsp whole juniper berries
30–60g/2–4 tbsp good-quality salt
1 litre/1¾ pints filtered water

1 Prepare the brine by melting the salt in the water. You might want to warm the water up a little to do this, but allow the brine to cool before using. The salt will help prevent a mushy cucumber.
2 Wash the cucumbers, carrot and horseradish well.
3 Slice the carrot into coins. The cucumbers can be left whole, if they are the small variety – or you can cut them into long slices or large chunks. Cut the horseradish into thin coins.
4 Put the vegetables in your clean fermentation jar together with the dill, leaves, mustard seeds and juniper berries.
5 Pour over the cooled-down brine, covering the cucumbers completely but with no excess water. You might not need to use all your brine.
6 Put a weight on top that keeps the cucumbers underneath the water. If you don't have a proper fermentation jar with weights I suggest you use the boiled stone or water-filled bag trick on page 39. Check regularly that the cucumbers are all underneath the water.
7 Leave the jar to ferment for 1–2 weeks in your kitchen. Put the jar on a plate as it ferments, as pickles tend to leak out a little. Don't forget to burp the jar once a day to let the gases out.
8 When done, transfer to the fridge. If a success these cucumbers will store for several months unopened.

For more guidance see the brine ferment instructions on page 49.

Green Beans with Dill

Fresh dill crowns are really yummy in any ferment and I use them a lot when in season. It can be difficult to get hold of unless you grow and pick them yourself, but of course you can use normal dill sprigs if you cannot get hold of the whole crowns. The flavour is different but both are nice.

Green beans are amazing vegetables, full of protein and easy to grow or get hold of through summer and autumn. Their nutrients disappear quickly after picking, but fermenting is a great way of holding onto the benefits. Eat this pickle like you would boiled green beans. It is lovely in salads and as a side dish.

1–1.5-LITRE/1¾–2½-PINT JAR

500g/1lb green beans
2 garlic cloves
5 dill crowns
15g/1 tbsp crushed chillies (optional, if you want some spice)
15–25g/1–1½ tbsp good-quality salt
500ml/17½fl oz filtered water

1 Make the brine by dissolving the salt in the water. You might want to warm the water up a little to do this. Allow the brine to cool down before using.
2 Wash the beans. I normally keep the beans whole, as they are. Peel the garlic cloves but keep them whole.
3 Put the beans in your clean fermentation jar by standing them up lengthwise. Add the garlic cloves and the dill, and crushed chilli if using, and make sure it is all packed in well.
4 Now pour the cooled-down brine over the beans to cover them completely but without excess water.
5 Put on a weight that keeps the beans underneath the water surface. If you don't have a proper fermentation jar with weights I suggest you use the boiled stone or water-filled bag trick on page 39. Check regularly that the beans are all underneath the water.
6 Leave the jar to ferment for 1–2 weeks at room temperature. Put on a plate as pickles tend to leak out a little. Don't forget to burp the jar once a day to let the gases out.
7 When done, transfer to the fridge. They will keep here for several months if unopened.

For more guidance see the brine ferment instructions on page 49.

C084141134

Sour Tomatoes with Rosemary and Thyme

Tomatoes are lovely to ferment whole with this pickling method. If you grow your own tomatoes you have probably noticed that all of a sudden you have more tomatoes than you can eat. Fermenting is a great way of preserving them. You can also use green tomatoes for this recipe or a combination of both green and red.

These fermented tomatoes are lovely to use in cooking. Make a tomato sauce with them, use as a base in soups and stews instead of canned tomatoes, make them into a raw salsa, passata or cultured ketchup – there are endless ways to use these tomatoes.

1.5-LITRE/2½-PINT JAR

1kg/2¼lb tomatoes
1 carrot
1 onion
4 garlic cloves
3 twigs of fresh thyme
3 sprigs of fresh rosemary
10g/2 tsp whole black peppercorns
30–45g/2–3 tbsp good-quality salt
1 litre/1¾ pints filtered water

1 Make the brine by dissolving the salt in the water. You might want to warm the water up a little to do this, but allow it cool before using.
2 Wash the tomatoes and carrot. Slice the carrot into coins. Peel the onion and chop roughly. Peel the garlic cloves and keep them whole.
3 Put the tomatoes, carrot and onion in your clean fermentation jar making sure they are well packed. Add the garlic cloves, thyme, rosemary and peppercorns.
4 Now pour the cooled-down brine over the tomatoes, covering them completely but with no excess water.
5 Put on a weight that keeps the tomatoes underneath the water. If you don't have a proper fermentation jar with weights I suggest you use the boiled stone or water-filled bag trick on page 39. Check regularly that the tomatoes are all underneath the water.
6 Leave the jar to ferment for 2–3 weeks at room temperature. Don't forget to burp the jar once a day to let the gases out.
7 When done, transfer to smaller jars if necessary and store in the fridge. This pickle will keep for a few months in the fridge if unopened.

For more guidance see the brine ferment instructions on page 49.

Mixed Pickles

You can use pretty much any vegetable you have to hand for this recipe. Try for example cauliflower, celery, garlic cloves, peppers, carrots and broccoli. Add herbs like dill, caraway seeds, mustard seeds, cumin and coriander. These pickles are a good accompaniment to most meals, as a digestive aid.

1kg/2¼lb mixed vegetables
30g/2 tbsp herbs of your choice
30–60g/2–4 tbsp good-quality salt
1 litre/1¾ pints filtered water

1.5-LITRE/2½-PINT JAR

1 Make the brine by melting the salt in the water. You might have to warm the water up a little to do this. Let cool.
2 Wash the vegetables and cut away any bad bits. Peel them if you need to. Cut the vegetables into your preferred size.
3 Put the vegetables into the clean fermentation jar, pressing them down as hard as possible without damaging them.
4 Now pour the cooled-down brine over the vegetables, covering them completely but with no excess water. You might not need all the water you have made up.
5 Now put on a weight to keep the vegetables underneath the water surface. If you don't have a proper fermentation jar with weights I suggest using the boiled stone or water-filled bag trick on page 39.
6 Leave the jar to ferment for 2 weeks at room temperature in your kitchen. Put on a plate as pickles tend to leak out a little. Don't forget to burp the jar once a day to let the gases out.
7 After 2 weeks, move to the fridge. Pickles improve when kept in the fridge for a while after being made. These will store for several months if unopened.

For more guidance see the brine ferment instructions on page 49.

Fermented Wild Garlic

Wow! I first tried fermented wild garlic at my local farmer's market. There is a stall selling fermented foods and they had experimented with fermenting wild garlic and it was just delicious. I immediately had to go and pick some for my own to ferment – where I live the countryside is absolutely overgrown with wild garlic in early spring so there is no shortage of it and it is free if you pick it yourself. Some farmer's markets and shops sell fresh wild garlic too.

This pickled vegetable is great to use as a flavouring in cooking, in a pesto sauce, in a mayonnaise, chopped up in an omelette, or served as a dip, just as it is.

250g/9oz wild garlic leaves
15g/1 tbsp good-quality salt
500ml/17½fl oz filtered water

300-ML/½-PINT JAR

1 Make the brine by dissolving the salt in the water. You might want to warm the water up a little to do this, just let it cool down before use.
2 Wash the wild garlic, and put them in a bowl with the cooled-down brine to soak for a while to make them more pliable. The leaves should become quite soft.
3 Put the leaves into a clean fermentation jar one by one, making sure they are tightly packed.
4 Pour over enough brine to cover the leaves. You will probably not need all the brine you made up.
5 You probably do not need to put a weight to keep the leaves underneath the water. The leaves normally stay where they are if soaked beforehand. If you find you need to I would suggest using the boiled stone or water-filled bag trick on page 39.
6 Leave the jar to ferment for 2 weeks at room temperature. Don't forget to burp the jar once a day to let the gases out.
7 When done, store in the fridge – this will keep for several months if unopened.

For more guidance see the brine ferment instructions on page 49.

Fermented Rhubarb

If you grow your own rhubarb you will have plenty of it and not know what to do with it all. Growing up in Sweden we had rhubarb coming out of our ears and we treated it like a weed rather than a gift of food. Now living in London, I don't grow rhubarb myself so I am relying on my friend Ben who has a beautiful allotment to give them to me. To ferment your rhubarb stalks is a wonderful way to make use of them. The sourness of the rhubarb actually turns milder when you ferment it. The whole chilli adds a kick.

This ferment is really tasty to use in a rhubarb crumble, and is great on top of your porridge or pot of yogurt, or kefir. It is also lovely as a relish with many dishes.

1–1.5-LITRE/1¾–2½-PINT JAR

500g/1lb rhubarb stalks
2–3 whole red chillies (optional)
15g/1 tbsp freshly grated ginger
15–20g/1–1¼ tbsp good-quality salt
500ml/17½fl oz filtered water

1 Make the brine by dissolving the salt in the water. You might want to warm the water up a little to do this but let it cool down before use.
2 Wash the rhubarb and cut the stalks up into the size you want. Leave the chillies as they are.
3 Put the rhubarb, whole chillies and grated ginger in your clean fermentation jar or jars. Pack them in tightly.
4 Pour the cooled-down brine over the rhubarbs, just enough to cover them completely.
5 Put on a weight that keeps the rhubarbs underneath the water. If you don't have a proper fermentation jar with weights I suggest using the boiled stone or water-filled bag trick on page 39.
6 Leave the jar to ferment for 1–2 weeks in your kitchen. The smaller the sticks of rhubarb, the shorter the fermentation process. Don't forget to burp the jar once a day to let the gases out.
7 When done, store in the fridge. This will keep for several months unopened.

For more guidance see the brine ferment instructions on page 49.

Pickled Chillies

I buy chillies from my local farmer's market and usually get bags full of them from the stallholder. If I end up with too many chillies in my fridge I will ferment them, and then use them to make the fantastic fermented chilli sauce on page 128. I usually pickle the chillies whole with the seeds, although perhaps I woud take out the seeds of Scotch Bonnet chillies as those are so extremely hot. Use these pickles as a hot accompaniment, chopped to spice up a dish, or to make the fiery chilli salsa.

1-LITRE/1¾-PINT JAR

500g/1lb fresh chillies
1 onion
5 garlic cloves
30g/2 tbsp good-quality salt
1 litre/1¾ pints filtered water

1 Make the brine by dissolving the salt in the water. You might want to warm the water up a little to do this, but allow it to cool down before using.
2 Wash the chillies and either keep them whole as they are, or if you want to ferment them without the seeds, halve them lengthwise and scrape out all the seeds and inner walls. Peel the onion and garlic, and chop them slightly.
3 Put the chillies, onion and garlic into your clean fermentation jar or jars, making sure they are well packed.
4 Pour in the cooled-down brine to cover them completely but with no excess water.
5 Now put on a weight that keeps the ingredients underneath the water. If you don't have a proper fermentation jar with weights I suggest you use the boiled stone or water-filled bag trick on page 39. Check regularly that everything remains underneath the water.
6 Leave the jar to ferment for 2–3 weeks in your kitchen, making sure to burp the jar once a day to let the gases out.
7 When done, store in the fridge. This will keep for several months unopened.

For more guidance see the brine ferment instructions on page 49.

CHAPTER FOUR:

Kimchi

Kimchi is a Korean sauerkraut that is very popular at the moment and rightly so. Kimchi is made from fermented cabbage along with various other vegetables like daikon and radishes as well as chillies, garlic and ginger, making it (very) spicy in flavour. By making it yourself you can decide on the level of heat and spiciness depending on your tastebuds, but if you buy a proper Korean kimchi it will be seriously spicy. Korean children are started on white kimchi, which is kimchi without chilli, then they are eased into the spiciness of chilli as they grow older. I try and get hold of the Korean chilli mix called Gochugaru – it can be found online and from Korean shops or Asian superstores. This mixture is very hot and sweet and will add a deep red colour to your kimchi. The hottest chillies are normally the Scotch Bonnet.

Traditionally, in Korean kimchi they use fermented fish sauce or fish or prawns, which you can choose to do or not. Either way will be delicious. Personally, I don't use fish sauce in my regular kimchi, but I have included a recipe with fish sauce although it is not a traditionally Korean recipe but an adapted one. When sourcing your fish sauce make sure it does not contain any preservatives as this can tamper with the ferment. Sugar and salt are often added to these sauces, which is fine, but preferably nothing else. If you do include fish sauce you should adjust the amount of additional salt used. It is worth noting here that traditional bought Korean kimchi can contain a very high amount of salt, which is why it is much better to make it yourself and control the level used.

Kimchi has a distinctive smell as well as taste. Most people love the taste of kimchi but are not always so delighted by the smell. If you make kimchi using fish sauce and dried shrimps it will smell even more. In a Korean kitchen, where they tend to eat kimchi daily with meals, home-owners often have special kimchi fridges so that the rest of their food will not be contaminated by the smell. When fermenting kimchi at home your kitchen can adopt this special scent so you might want to ferment it in a cupboard or something similar.

Kimchi, as with sauerkraut, contains brassicas which have the many health benefits mentioned earlier, including being excellent for the liver, anti-cancerous and anti-inflammatory. Daikon or mooli is also an amazing vegetable that is especially beneficial for your gut and digestion. It is also a chelator, anti-cancerous, anti-bacterial, anti-viral, brilliant decongestant, good for your kidneys, and an aid in weight loss. Daikon is high in prebiotics which makes it helpful for gut health as well as being rich in vitamins and minerals. In other words, very good for you, and worth this special mention!

Above: The name kimchi refers both to the spiced paste and to the fermented vegetable dish that incorporates it. Kimchi can be made successfully with all manner of vegetables, but traditionally includes Napa cabbage, radishes and carrots, as well as garlic, fresh ginger and of course chilli.

BASIC METHOD: Kimchi

Kimchi can be made using dry fermentation, but traditional kimchi is made by soaking the vegetables in salty water for several hours. This method is not dry-salt fermentation or brine fermentation; perhaps it can be described as in-between. In my opinion the following method is the best, and most similar to that used in a classic Korean recipe.

1 Making the brine. The kimchi brine should be fairly salty with 45–60g/1½–2oz or 3–4 tbsp of salt to every litre/1¾ pints of filtered water. It is easiest to warm a small amount of the water so that the salt melts and dissolves. However, a good-quality salt should dissolve fairly quickly. If heated up allow the brine to cool to room temperature before using.
2 Preparing the vegetables. Wash your vegetables, cutting away any bad bits, and chop up in the way you prefer. Traditionally kimchi cabbage is fermented in large pieces, sometimes not chopped up at all, but personally, I prefer it chopped fairly small. The traditional cabbage used in kimchi is Chinese cabbage or Napa cabbage, but normal white cabbage is also fine.
3 Brining the vegetables. Put all the chopped vegetables, but not the spices, in a large pot or bowl. Cover completely with the salty brine. To keep the vegetables below the water you can put a plate or other weight on top. Soak in the brine for 8 hours or overnight.
4 Straining the vegetables. After 8 hours, strain the vegetables, keeping back some of the liquid for the kimchi paste. Make sure the vegetables are well drained.
5 Making the kimchi paste. Blend together all the spices you are using in a blender or food processor, and include a small handful of soaked vegetables to make a thick smoothie consistency. You might also have to add a little bit of the soaking brine for the blades to go round. You want a creamy 'smoothie' consistency but not too runny. You can make batches of the paste to keep in the fridge and use when needed, of course.
6 Massaging the vegetables. In a large bowl, lightly massage the thick paste gently into the vegetables until they are all well covered. This is not like massaging the vegetables in a dry fermentation. The idea here is only to get the vegetables covered with the kimchi paste and not to break the vegetables down. They are already broken down by the soaking. This is easiest done by hand but make sure to wear gloves or use a utensil for this as it can be painful otherwise, with the chilli heat.
7 Packing the vegetables. Transfer the vegetables to your clean fermentation jar and pack them in tightly, making sure there are no air bubbles. This is not quite as important as when making sauerkraut as the spices will kill off any bacteria trying to enter the ferment – you don't have to add a protective cabbage leaf and weight to push down, but you can if you prefer. Leave a 5cm/2in gap for gases to be able to come out.
8 Fermenting. Let the jar ferment in your kitchen at room temperature for 2–3 weeks. Don't forget to burp the jar daily by opening the lid quickly to let the air out. Kimchi is quicker to ferment than sauerkraut; I normally transfer to the fridge after 2 weeks.
9 Storing. When done, you can transfer to smaller jars if necessary and store in the fridge. Unopened kimchi lasts for months.

Kimchi Paste

This paste is rarely exactly the same each time. The result varies with the chillies I use, and sometimes I add in more fresh vegetables, and less paprika powder. This is the beauty of fermenting; it is an art and actually difficult to make precisely the same ferment time after time.

The quantities in this recipe make enough paste for 1 batch of kimchi. You could use less if you wish, though I often double up to make larger batches as you see in the photographs – I usually do this when I know I have classes or workshops coming up as it stores well in the fridge for several weeks.

This paste can be used for cabbage kimchi, cucumber kimchi or indeed most any other type of kimchi.

30g/1oz fresh garlic cloves, peeled

60g/2oz fresh ginger root

50g/1¾oz good-quality paprika powder (use 10g smoked and 40g normal paprika powder for a deep smoky flavour)

2 fresh red chillies, deseeded

15g/1 tbsp (or more if you prefer) Korean chilli powder (Gochugaru) or other hot chilli powder

30ml/2 tbsp fish sauce, with no preservatives (optional, omit for vegetarians)

50ml/1¾fl oz liquid retained from a previous successful batch of kimchi, or use some retained soaking brine

15ml/1 tbsp apple cider vinegar

½ fresh red bell pepper

15ml/1 tbsp tamari or gluten-free soy sauce

45g/3 tbsp coconut sugar

300-ML/½-PINT JAR

1 Put all the ingredients in a blender or food processor and blend to a good thick paste consistency, adding liquid as you need either from the vegetable soaking water if you have some, liquid from a previous batch of kimchi, or filtered water.

2 Test and adjust the spices to suit your taste.

3 Use the paste for your kimchi straight away or store in a clean glass jar in the fridge. It will keep for several weeks.

Top tip! If you have a previous batch of kimchi, add some to the new paste for flavour. This is often done in traditional kimchi recipes.

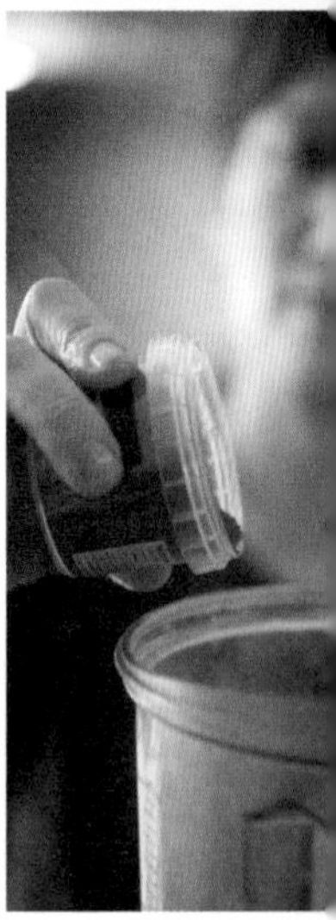

Åsa's Kimchi

Kimchi is lovely with any dish. Awesome with meat or veggie burgers and hot dogs, it works amazingly well with pulled pork dishes or similar vegan alternatives, and is great in a stir-fry and with noodles. Sometimes kimchi can get a little mushy. If that happens I use it in cooking, adding it to soups and stews where it gives a wonderful umami flavour.

1.5-LITRE/2½-PINT JAR

60–75g/2–2½oz good-quality salt
1.5 litres/2½ pints filtered water
1kg/2¼lb (about 1 large) Chinese or Napa cabbage
250g/9oz (about 1 small) daikon radish or mooli
3 medium carrots
5 radishes
1 spring onion/scallion
50–75g/1¾–2½oz kimchi paste (see page 106)

1 Make the brine by dissolving the salt in the water. If heated up, allow to cool to room temperature, and pour into a large bowl or pot.
2 Wash the vegetables and cut off any bad bits.
3 Chop the cabbage; you can cut into fairly large pieces. In traditional recipes they often just divide the cabbage in half or quarters or even put the whole cabbage to soak; I like smaller pieces but not as thin as in sauerkraut-making. Chop the daikon and carrots into thin coins or grate them; thinly slice the radishes into coins; and chop the spring onion into small circles.
4 Put all the vegetables in the brine, making sure they are submerged under the water surface. Put a plate on top to keep the vegetables submerged. Let the vegetables soak overnight or for 8 hours.
5 Strain the water from the vegetables, keeping some of the brine in case you need it for the kimchi paste. Make sure they are well drained and put them into a mixing bowl.
6 Make the kimchi paste if not already made.
7 Lightly massage the kimchi paste by hand with gloves so the paste covers the vegetables all over. Use a wooden spoon or other implement if you have no gloves. I made the mistake of not wearing gloves once, and will not make that mistake again!
8 Pack tightly into your clean fermentation jar, making sure you have at least 5cm/2in at top to spare for the vegetables to expand and gases to escape.
9 Put on a weight if needed to keep the vegetables tightly packed, using one of the tricks on pages 38–9. If using a proper fermentation jar you can use the weight included. It is not as important to submerge the kimchi as with sauerkraut. This is because of the strong spices which also help to keep unwanted bacteria away. The consistency of the water should not be very watery but more like a smoothie.
10 Let ferment at room temperature for 2–3 weeks. In my experience, it is ready after 2 weeks.
11 When ready, transfer to smaller jars if necessary and store in the fridge. It will keep for several months if unopened.

For more guidance see the basic kimchi instructions on page 104.

Cucumber Kimchi

This recipe is delicious. Kimchi cucumbers are great to accompany any meal; I use them on sandwiches, in rolls, kebabs and falafels, and this always appears as part of the Swedish Christmas smorgasbord in our house. The carrot is added to stop the cucumber from going mushy – see the Swedish cucumber pickle recipe on page 87 for more information regarding this trick.

1.5-LITRE/2½-PINT JAR

1kg/2¼lb cucumbers (English or Kirby)
1 small carrot
20g/1¼ tbsp good-quality salt
40g/3 tbsp kimchi paste (see page 106)

1 Prepare the cucumbers, washing them and slicing them to your preferred size. Chop the carrot into coins.
2 Put the vegetables in a glass mixing bowl, add the salt and stir. Leave overnight or for 10 hours for the water to be drawn out of the cucumbers. This will become the natural brine for the ferment.
3 After 10 hours, strain the vegetables but keep the water back in case you need it for the kimchi paste.
4 Make the kimchi paste if not already made.
5 Add the kimchi paste to the strained vegetables and mix together well. You might choose to add some of the cucumber liquid to make the paste a little runnier; I like to do this.
6 Transfer the vegetables to your clean fermentation jar, making sure they are submerged under the water surface. You might need to use a weight to push them down – see pages 38–9 for suggestions.
7 Let ferment at room temperature for 1–2 weeks.
8 When done, transfer to smaller jars if necessary and store in the fridge. Cucumber kimchi stores well if the cucumbers are of good quality and of the varieties suggested; otherwise, you may find they go mushy within a few weeks so eat them up soon.

Curried Kimchi

I love the texture and consistency of kimchi and was wondering if I could add some Indian spices rather than Korean spices and make a curry-style kimchi (I am always experimenting with various spices for my kimchi). This recipe worked out really well, and is a good accompaniment to many meals but especially curries and other Indian dishes; it is great added to a dosa. Yum!

1.5-LITRE/2½-PINT JAR

- 45g/1½oz good-quality salt
- 1 litre/1¾ pints filtered water
- 500g/1lb cauliflower
- 300g/10½oz white cabbage
- 200g/7oz carrots
- 3 garlic cloves, peeled
- 4cm/1½in piece of fresh ginger
- 30–45g/2–3 tbsp garam masala (homemade if possible)
- 5–10g/1–2 tsp cayenne pepper
- 5g/1 tsp ground turmeric

1 Make the brine by dissolving the salt in the water. If heated up, cool to room temperature, and pour into a large bowl or pot.
2 Wash and prepare the cauliflower, cabbage and carrots, cutting away any bad bits and peeling the carrots. Grate the cauliflower and carrots coarsely and thinly julienne the cabbage.
3 Put all the prepared vegetables into the brine, making sure they are under the water. Put a plate on top to keep them submerged. Let the vegetables soak overnight or for 8 hours. Do not put the spices in with them yet.
4 Strain the water from the vegetables, keeping back a little brine in case it is needed to add to the paste later, and make sure they are well drained. Put them into a mixing bowl.
5 Make a curry kimchi paste by blending a little (about 100g/3½oz) of the soaked vegetables with the garlic, ginger and all the ground spices, mixing into a smoothie paste and adding water from the salty brine if needed.
6 Lightly massage the paste into the vegetables by hand so that it covers them all over.
7 Pack tightly into your clean fermentation jar, making sure you have at least 5cm/2in spare for the vegetables to expand and the gases to escape.
8 Make sure a weight is keeping the vegetables tightly packed and submerged underneath the water surface using one of the tricks on pages 38–9. If you are using a proper fermentation jar you can use the weight included.
9 Let ferment at room temperature for 2–3 weeks. Burp the jar daily to release the gases.
10 When done, transfer to smaller jars if necessary and store in the fridge. This kimchi will keep for several months if unopened.

For more guidance see the basic kimchi instructions on page 104.

Mooli Kimchi

Mooli or daikon radish is high in prebiotics and lends itself beautifully to a successful ferment. This recipe is an adaptation of a Korean kimchi called Kkakdugi; traditionally a Korean radish rather than mooli is used but they are very similar so any could be used successfully. I prefer to prepare the mooli by slicing it thinly on a mandoline but you could also cut it into small cubes.

1.5-LITRE/2½-PINT JAR

30g/2 tbsp good-quality salt
600ml/1 pint filtered water
1kg/2¼lb mooli, daikon or Korean radish
small bunch of spring onions/scallions
5 garlic cloves, chopped finely
30g/2 tbsp grated fresh ginger root
30ml/2 tbsp tamari
30g/2 tbsp coconut sugar
30g/2 tbsp of either fresh chopped red chilli or dried Korean chilli powder (Gochuraku)
15g/1 tbsp sesame seeds (optional)
5ml/1 tsp toasted sesame oil (optional)

1 Make a brine by dissolving the salt in the water. You might need to heat it up slightly, then set aside to cool down.
2 Prepare the mooli by washing and peeling if necessary. Slice the mooli fairly thinly using a mandoline or a knife. I like thin slices (the kimchi is good in a burger!) but it doesn't really matter; if you prefer you can cut it into cubes.
3 Chop the spring onions into thin round slices.
4 Transfer the mooli and spring onion to a mixing bowl and then pour the brine over the vegetables and leave to soak for a few hours or overnight.
5 Pour out the brine from the mooli mix but keep back some of the liquid in a jug for later. The vegetables are still in a mixing bowl but now without the water.
6 Now, add the chopped garlic, grated ginger, tamari, sugar and chilli powder, as well as sesame seeds and oil if using. Use protective gloves to mix together with your hands, making sure it's blended well. Add a little bit of the salty brine if needed.
7 Transfer the mooli mix to your clean fermentation jar. Press the vegetables firmly down, still wearing your gloves. The vegetables should be covered with liquid. Add some more of the salty brine if needed.
8 Leave at room temperature to ferment for 2–3 weeks. Remember to burp the jar daily for the first week.
9 When ready, transfer to smaller jars if necessary and store in the fridge. It will last for several months in the fridge if unopened.

For more guidance see the basic kimchi instructions on page 104.

Korean Kimchi with Fish Sauce

Traditional kimchi is not vegetarian, or vegan. It contains fish sauce, and dried fish or shrimps. These ingredients are themselves salted, so added to the salt in the brine or ferment itself, Korean kimchi is often extremely salty. This is not good for bowel health and on top of that too much salt kills off even the good bacteria. So, I am careful with traditional kimchi recipes and reduce the salt as much as possible. This version of kimchi is done in a slightly different way from the traditional soaking recipe, but it works very well. This is a recipe used at the Natural Chef programme I teach at The London College of Naturopathic Medicine.

1-LITRE/1¾-PINT JAR

800g/1¾lb Chinese or Napa cabbage (around 1 large head)

1–2 medium carrots

¼ medium mooli or daikon radish

4 radishes

5cm/2in fresh ginger root

4 garlic cloves

bunch of spring onions/scallions, chopped

15g/1 tbsp good-quality salt

10g/2 tsp dried Korean chilli powder (Gochuraku)

15ml/1 tbsp fish sauce (Nam Pla)

1 Wash the cabbages or remove the outer leaves if they are damaged. You might want to peel the carrots and mooli, but is not necessary if they are fresh and organic.
2 Chop the cabbage fairly small as this is a recipe that we need to massage slightly. Grate the carrots and the mooli, and slice the radishes finely. Then add all to a mixing bowl.
3 Grate the fresh ginger and chop the garlic small. Slice the spring onions thinly. Set aside, separate from the other vegetables for now.
4 Add the salt to the cabbage mix, stir around and let sit for 15 minutes for osmosis (movement of water) to happen. You probably only need to massage it slightly as Chinese cabbage is soft and will not need much work for the water to come out.
5 When your vegetables look slightly cooked and you can see the water coming out then add the rest of the ingredients, including the spring onion, ginger and garlic, and the chilli and fish sauce.
6 Stir and massage again only lightly so that everything is mixed together well and the spices and herbs are on all the vegetables.
7 Transfer the kimchi to your clean fermentation jar, packing it in tightly with your fist or a pounder so that the vegetables are underneath the water surface with no hidden air bubbles. If there is not enough water to cover the vegetables, add some filtered water. Leave around 5cm/2in from the surface of water to the lid of the jar, for the gases to come out.
8 Put a weight on the vegetables to keep them under the water surface using one of the suggested ways on pages 38–9.
9 Let the kimchi ferment at room temperature for 2–3 weeks. Check regularly that the vegetables are underneath the water. If you do not use a proper fermentation crockpot or specific fermentation lid, don't forget to burp the jar once a day to let the gases out; this means to quickly open the lid to let the air out and then close it.
10 When the ferment is ready, transfer to smaller jars if necessary and store in the fridge. It will keep for several months if unopened.

For more guidance see the basic kimchi instructions on page 104 as well as the dry-salt ferment instructions on page 44.

Le Parfait
FAMILIA WISS®
KILNER®
EST 1842

CHAPTER FIVE:

Fermented Fruits and Sauces

Fruits can also be fermented, although less commonly so than vegetables; they are perhaps not as useful as vegetables but can still be delicious and interesting. There are a few differences when comparing with vegetables. Firstly, most fruits ferment much more quickly than vegetables and cannot be left in room temperature for weeks, as they will go off. Secondly, most fruits cannot be stored anywhere else than in the fridge and even inside the fridge, they will not keep for long; a few weeks or perhaps a couple of months at the most. Thirdly, unlike vegetables, fruits need a starter to get going, because they are much sweeter, and they can go off before they start to ferment. Most fruit ferments are therefore cultured rather than wild-fermented.

Fermenting a fruit will retain its nutrients as well as adding beneficial bacteria. The sugar content will also be much lower as this will be transformed by the healthy lactic acid bacteria. There are fewer studies on fermented fruit, but the general thoughts are that the amazing health benefits of fermented foods might not all apply to fruit ferments. However, it is still a great way of getting some probiotics as well as all the nutrients that the raw fruit or berry will provide.

For the fruit fermentation recipes in this book I use probiotic powder (from a capsule) as a starter but you might want to use one of the other starters that are listed on page 32. They should all work well in fruit fermentation. Probiotic powder contains one or several strains of lactic acid bacteria and will help kickstart the ferment as well as control it slightly, as you can decide yourself what strain of bacteria you would like to add. For the fermentation process it does not matter what strain of bacteria you choose but if you have certain health issues you might want to be specific. For example Saccharomyces boulardii (which is actually a kind of yeast but works well) is considered to be good for Candida, Lactobacillus plantarum is good to heal leaky gut, whilst Lactobacillus acidophilus is helpful for IBS.

The fermentation process is normally quick, especially in warm weather. They can easily over-ferment and become gassy due to the high natural sugar content, so you need to check your fruit ferment almost daily to make sure this doesn't happen. If it gets very bubbly with a sharp fermented taste, you have left it for too long and although it is safe to eat it may not be very nice-tasting. Take it early rather than later, as it will continue to ferment slightly even when in the fridge.

Once fermented fruits are ready and stored in a refrigerator, they need to be eaten within a few weeks. I have kept fruit ferments for a few months in the past in the fridge, and they have sometimes been fine to use, but be aware that this might not be the case for you. When jars of fruit ferment are opened and you have started to eat them, they generally last only for a couple of weeks. Saying this, there are exceptions, and some fruits in this chapter do require a longer fermentation – the preserved lemons for example will only get better and better with time, and can continue to ferment for as long as a couple of years.

Tomato and Coriander Salsa

Tomato is technically a fruit, and this specific recipe requires a starter so is included here and not in the vegetable section. This salsa is a wonderful-tasting fermented sauce and if treated with care it will last for several months in your fridge. Use just as you would any other salsa sauce, as a dip or a condiment. It is excellent with tacos and other Mexican food.

1-LITRE/1¾-PINT JAR

750g/1½lb tomatoes
½ green bell pepper
small bunch of fresh coriander/cilantro
½ red onion
1 garlic clove
1 spring onion/scallion
½ fresh green or red chilli (depending what strength you want in your salsa)
30ml/2 tbsp raw apple cider vinegar
15g/1 tbsp cumin seeds
5–10g/1–2 tsp good-quality salt
1 probiotic capsule (content only)

1 Wash the tomatoes, green pepper and herbs. Peel the onion and garlic.
2 Dice the tomatoes, green pepper, onion and spring onion, to your preferred salsa size. Chop the coriander and chilli small. Grate the garlic.
3 Combine all the fresh ingredients in a mixing bowl with the vinegar, cumin seeds and salt, and mix by hand.
4 Take half of the mixture out and put into a blender or food processor, and blend to a purée. Return the purée back to the mixing bowl with the rest of the salsa and stir together well. This stage is optional but will give you more of a salsa texture.
5 Add the content of the probiotic capsule to the salsa, and stir.
6 Place the mixture into your clean fermentation jar. There should be enough liquid to cover, and for this ferment there is no need to put any weights on it, just make sure there are no air bubbles. Make sure there is 5cm/2in space left below the jar opening for gases to escape into.
7 Let the salsa ferment in your kitchen for 3–5 days. Burp it daily if you remember. The tomatoes will begin to separate from the liquid when it is ready. Stir and taste it on the third day – if it is already slightly bubbly and tasty, move it straight to the fridge.
8 It is best to decant your salsa into smaller jars when ready, then unopened the jars will last for at least 2 months in your fridge. If opened use up within a couple of weeks.

Cultured Spicy Ketchup

This is a great condiment with a natural and spicy sweet taste. It is a super-healthy alternative to commercial ketchup, which usually contains high-fructose corn syrup, excessive sugar and salt. In this recipe, I suggest using canned or bottled tomato purée but if you prefer you can make your own, from fresh tomatoes that you have boiled down to a purée. Making your own is of course nicer but it takes longer to do. You can also use the brine-fermented whole tomatoes (see page 91) and blend the tomatoes when finished. Use this as you would a normal ketchup; it is also good as a dip, and stirred into other sauces.

300g/10½oz organic tomato purée or paste (about 1 jar or 2 small cans)
60ml/2fl oz or 4 tbsp maple syrup
30ml/2 tbsp raw apple cider vinegar
1 probiotic capsule (content only)
1 garlic clove, peeled and crushed
pinch ground cloves
2.5g/½ tsp onion powder
2.5g/½ tsp ground cinnamon
pinch allspice
pinch cumin
pinch cayenne pepper
pinch ground black pepper
pinch sea salt
50ml/1¾fl oz filtered water (if needed)

600-ML/1-PINT JAR

1 Combine all the ingredients apart from the water, and stir to combine well, tasting and adjusting the spices as needed. You may or may not want to then add a bit of water depending on how thick your purée is.
2 Transfer to your clean fermenting jar, making sure there are no air bubbles in the mixture.
3 Leave to ferment at room temperature for 2–5 days, checking after 2. Unless you have a fermentation jar you need to briefly open the lid daily to burp or let the gases out.
4 Taste to test and when the fermented sauce is to your liking, put the ketchup in the fridge for another 2–3 days and then it is ready to enjoy. This fermented ketchup should last up to 3 months in your fridge unopened; when opened use within a few weeks.

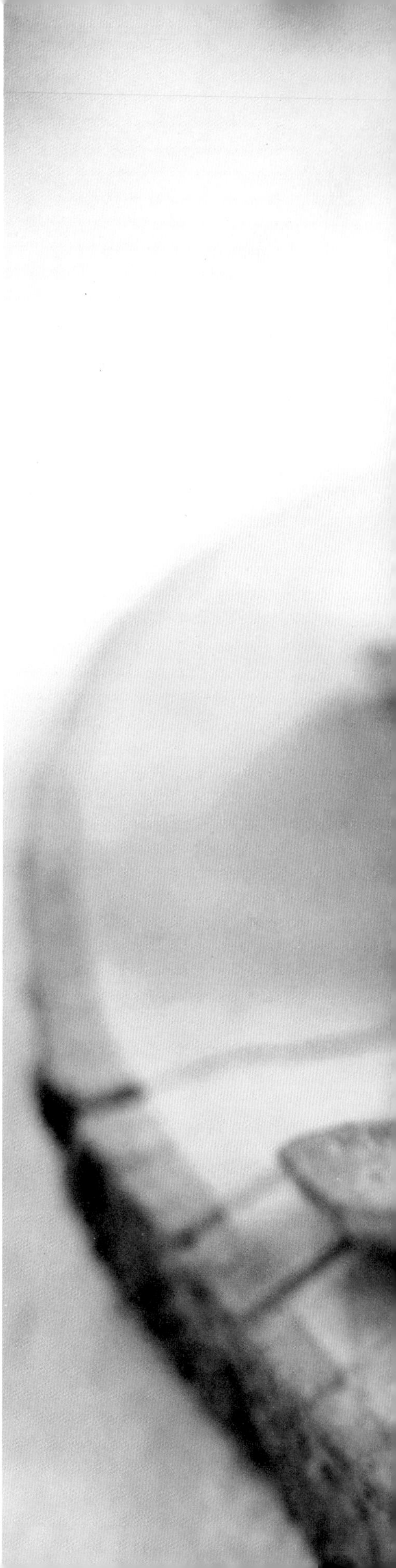

Spicy Pear and Pecan Chutney

My family love this fruit ferment recipe and I have adapted it over time. In my workshops, I always serve this together with nut cheeses and most of my students love it. I even had to supply a students' café with this chutney until the owner had taught her chefs how to make it. My kids have it on their porridge as a spicy jam, and it works well as a dessert on its own with some cream or spooned on top of a cake.

1-LITRE/1¾-PINT JAR

750g/1½lb ripe pears
100g/3½oz goji berries or raisins
100g/3½oz chopped pecan nuts
30g/2 tbsp finely grated ginger
250g/9oz fresh or soaked dates
100–200ml/3½ –7fl oz filtered water (as needed)
30g/2 tbsp ground cinnamon
5g/1 tsp good-quality salt
2 probiotic capsules (content only)

1 Wash the ripe pears and core them and cut out any bad bits. You can peel and core them if you wish or leave the peel on, it works well both ways – I tend to do half with skin and half without. Dice the pears into 1 x 1cm/½ x ½in cubes or your preferred size.
2 Put the diced pears in a mixing bowl and add the goji berries, chopped pecan nuts and grated ginger, and mix well.
3 Put the dates into a blender together with half the water to start with, and process to a paste. Add the cinnamon and salt to the slightly runny paste and blend well, adding more water if you need to. Add the probiotic at the end, stirring carefully to mix it well.
4 Pour the date paste over the pears and mix well.
5 Transfer the pear chutney to your clean fermentation jar, packing the chutney in well to get rid of any air bubbles. The paste should cover the pears, but if it doesn't mix in a little bit more water. If a weight will help then use this, otherwise there is no need for weights in this ferment.
6 Leave at room temperature to ferment for 2–4 days, checking it daily so it doesn't over-ferment. This chutney tends to ferment from the bottom up, so check the bottom of the ferment rather than the top to see if it is done or not. You can stir it for this reason when you check.
7 When done, transfer to the fridge immediately. If stored well in clean jars without opening the chutney might last for 2 months in the fridge. Otherwise eat up within a week or two.

Spicy Chilli Salsa

This is the perfect use for the brine-fermented chillies you pickled earlier (see page 98). It's a simple spicy hot sauce with all the additional nutritional benefits a ferment can bring as well as the health benefits of the chillies themselves. Chillies are known to help with pain and prevent colds and flus, are good for weight loss, and improve the metabolism. Use this salsa just as you would any other chilli sauce – as a spice in cooking, a condiment and a dip. The chillies are pretty hot but fermenting makes them slightly milder somehow.

You can choose to make this sauce with just the fermented chillies and garlic cloves. It is delicious just like this, or you can add sugar, salt and other spices to flavour it. Use the salsa as a base for sweet chilli sauce or for a healthy version of sriracha.

1-LITRE/1¾-PINT JAR

batch of pickled chillies (see page 98)
100g/3½oz coconut sugar or agave syrup
5g/1 tsp salt
15ml/1 tbsp apple cider vinegar

1 Put the fermented chillies, including the garlic and onion from the jar, in a blender. You probably do not really need the brine for the sauce as it will be a perfect consistency anyway, without any added liquid. I do normally take away the stalks of the chillies but you don't need to.
2 Add the rest of the ingredients to the blender if you are using them.
3 Blend to the preferred consistency, which will not take long to achieve.
4 Salsa done! Pour it into a jar with a lid and store it in the fridge. This sauce will keep for several months if unopened.

Fermented Berry Jam

Berries do not contain much sugar, so it is hard to create a good berry ferment without adding something sugary for the bacteria to feed on. You can add any carbohydrate-rich sweetener of your choice to make a jam. Sugar, maple syrup, raw agave syrup, coconut sugar or date paste are all good sweeteners to use. Honey might work but would not be my first choice as it is anti-bacterial.

This is a classic Swedish jam (we call it queen's jam), using mixed wild blueberries, also known as bilberries, and wild raspberries from the Scandinavian forests. Scandinavian forest berries are very small and sweet and have an especially good flavour due to the long days of sunshine in the summer. You can only get these particular berries in Nordic countries but the recipe works well with berries from other countries too, and you can use fresh or frozen berries. My grandmother used to make this jam for us as children and eating it brings back many memories from our summers with her. It goes off quickly so do not make huge batches of it. I often make this jam raw, but I find it keeps better if you pasteurise it lightly. It also gives the jam a slightly less sharp taste if you cook it.

300-ML/½-PINT JAR

150g/5¼oz blueberries
150g/5¼oz raspberries
80–100ml/2¾–3½fl oz raw agave syrup
2.5g/½ tsp good-quality salt
1 probiotic capsule (content only)

1 Combine the berries, agave syrup and salt in a saucepan. Cook for 5 minutes at a low simmer, squashing the fresh berries lightly as they cook if they are fresh, to allow the juices to release. If they are frozen, the juices are available already without squashing them. Remove from the heat and set aside to cool.

2 Once cooled, empty the probiotic capsule powder into the mixture and stir in well.

3 Transfer to your clean fermentation jar. No weight is needed for this ferment.

4 Allow the jam to ferment at room temperature for about 2–3 days. You might have to open the lid to let gases out, though normally there is not much gas created.

5 When it is done, transfer to the fridge. If unopened, this jam will last for a month at least. Otherwise if opened use within 5 days. If you find this jam is too runny, add a tablespoon of chia seeds and stir well to thicken it.

Preserved Lemons

I tried these fermented lemons at my friend Bruna's place. She had made them and then left them untouched in a glass container on her kitchen bench, amongst other delightful jars of goodies, so this ferment was two years old when I tried it, and it was delicious. Very intense in flavour and very salty, so you can only use a little bit of it. Great as a seasoning to any food, I use fermented lemons in Middle Eastern or Asian dishes, in hummus, in broths and soups as well as stews and curries. Most Moroccan recipes for preserved lemons suggest a fermentation period of only 6 weeks. However, listening to various Moroccan fermenters as well as my friend Bruna, they all seem to agree that a year is a good time. If you are like me then you will not be able to wait for this long, but try and do what Bruna did and put it away and forget about it for a while. Believe me, it is worth the wait.

1-LITRE/1¾-PINT JAR

10 organic unwaxed lemons (or more if you wish), to preserve, plus additional lemons for the juice

10g/2 tsp good-quality salt for each preserved lemon

1 You need to cut into your lemons but try and keep them whole. Either start from the top and cut a cross almost all the way down so the lemon is still intact in one piece. Or you can cut a cross at the top and the bottom of the lemon, going almost to the middle so the lemon is still joined. However if the lemon ends up in several pieces don't worry, it will still work. If the lemon stays in one piece it is more likely to keep its yellow colour for longer and looks nice, that is all.

2 Pack 2 tsp of salt into each lemon. More salt might be needed but don't use less salt for this ferment.

3 Then put the lemons into the clean fermentation jar. Use your hands or a utensil to press them down so that the salt and the lemons create a natural brine that covers the lemon. If there is not enough liquid after some time of pressing and mashing (add more salt if necessary as it helps with osmosis), squeeze in additional lemons until their juice eventually covers the whole lemons. Do not add water to this ferment.

4 Leave the lemons to ferment at room temperature for at least 6 weeks. However, leaving them for longer is even better. You could try the lemons after 6 weeks and if you love them as they are, put them in the fridge and it will stop the ferment. If you have the patience and you want to create something special, leave it to ferment for longer. This ferment, if done correctly, will last for years.

CHAPTER SIX:

Fermented Drinks

I have eaten sauerkraut and other fermented vegetables as well as fermented dairy all my life, but fermented probiotic drinks are fairly new to me. I had rejuvelac as a little girl, but I had never heard of kombucha and kefir water until the year 2006 on a raw food retreat in the English countryside. I was blown away by both, and loved what they did to my digestive health. Since then, there is always a probiotic drink brewing in my kitchen. Kombucha and water kefir are staples but I also experiment with kvasses and rejuvelac. My family loves fermented drinks, and you will find that children don't need fizzy soft drinks when there are these great-tasting alternatives.

Kombucha is a fermented, naturally sparkling drink with a very pleasant taste. It is becoming extremely popular, and rightly so, as it is full of probiotics, antioxidants and beneficial enzymes. Its origin is unclear but kombucha is usually thought to have come from China, spreading to Japan and west through Russia and Eastern Europe. It has traditionally been used for a huge range of disorders and has been hailed a wonder drink by many people. Wonder drink or not, it is a most pleasant beverage for all ages to enjoy.

Water kefir is another probiotic-rich drink with a huge number of bacterial strains, making it a fantastic general probiotic. It will boost your immune system and look after your gut. If you have children that are either constipated or have diarrhoea then this drink will help them. Water kefir is included here but there is also milk kefir, of course, which is covered in the chapter on fermented dairy (and coconut milk kefir, in the non-dairy chapter).

If you don't have kombucha or water kefir starters, there are other drinks in this chapter you can experiment with at home. The starters used in these drinks are easier to get hold of online, or you can make them yourself.

Rejuvelac is made from the soak water of sprouted wheat berries and other grains. The drink was made famous in the 1970s by raw food and health pioneer Ann Wigmore, who claimed this drink was part of the protocol that cured her of cancer. Rejuvelac is full of natural probiotics and will help promote the beneficial bacteria in your gut to improve your overall health. The taste is light and pleasant with a slight sharp or tart flavour, a little like lemon, though the taste depends on what grain you choose to sprout.

Kvass is originally a fermented health drink from Russia and Eastern Europe. Traditionally it is made using stale rye bread. However, the word kvass is now also used to describe other sour fermented drinks. For example, tea kvass is another word for kombucha. You can be creative in making kvasses and use all kinds of berries, fruit, herbs and spices. The kvass recipes here are mainly made with fruit but there is also one traditional version using stale rye bread.

Some people ask if these fermented drinks contain alcohol, the answer is a trace; they are considered to be free of alcohol as the content is well under 0.5%, though the amount varies slightly depending on the fermentation. Of course, even a ripe fruit or fresh orange juice has a trace of alcohol.

All these drink recipes are good to have with your meals instead of water or juice as they will help with the digestion of the food you are eating, as well as helping you to take up the nutrients more efficiently. However, to get the most health benefits from fermented probiotic drinks, you should drink them on an empty stomach.

BASICS: Kombucha

Kombucha is the result of a fermentation process combining tea and sugar with a specific community of bacteria and yeast, also referred to as a SCOBY (Symbiotic Culture Of Bacteria and Yeast) or a 'mother'. The bacteria and yeast from the scoby work together in balance to ferment and convert the sugar and tea solution into the final kombucha drink. It is the scoby, which looks somewhat like a pancake or a jellyfish, that simply converts a sugary tea solution over a period of 1–3 weeks into a health-promoting beverage that contains many organic acids, active enzymes, amino acids, beneficial bacteria, probiotic microorganisms and polyphenols as well as many B-vitamins and vitamin C.

You can flavour your kombucha in creative ways. After the first initial fermentation, you can choose to do a second fermentation and add fruit and berries, herbs and spices for extra flavour and sweetness. The kombucha recipes in this book are my favourites but you can experiment. Some of my students have brought me the most fantastic kombuchas to taste, made with all kinds of unexpected ingredients.

During some work I did in Georgia, USA, I met an amazing woman with her own kombucha business. She made me this gorgeous brew of natural kombucha and apple cider mixed into a refreshing sangria-type drink. She cut up fresh fruit and mixed it with frozen berries and fresh mint leaves, and combined it with the kombucha brew. This was delicious, and beat any alcohol-laden beverage.

If you leave your kombucha to brew for too long it will taste like vinegar. Sometimes I do this, but I do not throw this brew away, I use it as vinegar. I have recently seen 'kombucha vinegar' being sold very expensively. Well this is how they make it; they over-ferment the kombucha brew!

SCOBY. This is Symbiotic Culture Of Bacteria and Yeast, and is the kombucha culture that you need in order to make the fermented drink. It is also referred to as a kombucha mushroom or a mother. It is described as a mother because it has babies. This sounds very strange, but with almost every kombucha batch the mother scoby will multiply and create a mini scoby. You can then peel this new scoby off, which will grow and have its own babies, and so on.

To start, you need to buy or get given a kombucha scoby. Once your scoby starts multiplying, the extra scobies can be given away to friends, be sold, make apparently very good face packs, be stretched and dried and used for something to draw on, dried to make a fabric, or boiled to make sweets. These surprising ideas are actual examples of what people have done with their excess scobies rather than throwing them away! When you don't use your scoby, store it

Below: The tea you use will have a huge impact on the flavour of your kombucha. I usually use green tea and the better quality you use, the better your kombucha will taste. My favourite is green tea with jasmine. Start off with cheaper tea and when you feel confident in your kombucha-making you can start experimenting with more sophisticated teas. Opposite: Here you see the scoby, the magic ingredient of kombucha.

in the fridge in a glass jar with some sweetened tea. It can be stored for months but it does prefer to be used and fed continuously.

Tea. You can make kombucha from any tea that contains caffeine as this is what the scoby likes to eat. Green tea, black tea or white tea all work. Different teas like different brewing temperatures – black tea can be brewed in boiling water but green tea prefers a lower temperature of 85–90°C/185–194°F. You can mix these teas with herbal teas, but it doesn't work with only herbal teas. Also, avoid teas flavoured with essential oils, such as Earl Grey tea, as it can damage your scoby. My favourites are matcha green tea, and green tea mixed with jasmine tea. The better-quality tea you use, the nicer-tasting your kombucha will be. You can also use coffee to make kombucha, or cola nuts as these contain caffeine.

Sugar. I tend to use organic granulated white sugar as this seems to work the best for my scoby. But results can vary a little so do try it out with your own preferred sugar. Generally, the darker the sugar the less well it works. I have tried using other sweeteners like coconut sugar and honey; however, although it works once or twice, it will stop working after a while, which suggests that scoby does need sugar to feed on properly. White sugar is stripped of any minerals so perhaps this is the reason it works better. My research suggests that scobies prefer as few minerals as possible to be present. Nonetheless, I have had students who swear that coconut sugar and date syrup work very well for their scoby. If you want to try out anything other than white or golden sugar I suggest you do a few batches first so that you have a few spare scobies to experiment with.

When I run my workshops, students often ask me if they can use something else than sugar, or if they can reduce the sugar, or even do it without sugar. The answer to this is basically No. The scoby needs to feed on sugar and is a vital part of the fermentation process. The sugar is not for you, it is for the scoby – the finished kombucha will not have much sugar left as this will have been eaten by the scoby and turned into acids and gases, which is what fermentation is all about.

Water. Filtered tap water or bottled still spring water is best. You do need to filter the water to remove the chlorine, as this disturbs the fermentation process. See page 30 for more information.

Fermentation jar. This can be any shape and size. No lid is used when making kombucha, just a cotton cloth. Kombucha needs oxygen to flow on top so putting it into a cupboard is not a good idea either. Do not use metal jars as the acidity of the kombucha may corrode the metal. Plastic is not good to use as this may leach chemicals into the kombucha. Good-quality glass, ceramic or clay jars are the best to use. As usual, clean your jars and hands well before doing any kind of food preparation. There should be no need to sterilise the jars for home brewing; however, should you want to, this is fine as long as no chemicals are used in the process.

Cotton cloth. Preferably organic muslin, this is to cover the jar instead of a lid. This makes it possible for the kombucha to breathe without getting dust or flies inside. Tie some string around it or use an elastic band.

Litmus paper. If you are unsure about how long to ferment your kombucha, you could use litmus to measure the pH level. It should be ready when the pH is around 3–3.2. pH measures how acidic a substance is. 7 is neutral; anything under 7 is acidic or sour, whilst over 7 is alkaline or basic.

Left: I find it is best to start a new brew immediately and get into a rhythm of making kombucha. If for some reason you want a break, you can store the scoby in some sweetened tea in the fridge. It will keep well for several weeks.

Simple Kombucha

This method is for a simple, natural kombucha which is not flavoured with anything. Use this as a base for the other recipes in the chapter.

2.5-LITRE/4½-PINT JAR

2 litres/3½ pints filtered water
15g/1 tbsp loose tea or 5 teabags
250g/9oz organic white granulated sugar
250ml/9fl oz previous batch of kombucha – or 30ml/2 tbsp of raw apple cider vinegar if it is your first batch
1 kombucha scoby

1 Heat up your measured filtered water in a pan to a good brewing temperature. As explained previously, this temperature depends on what tea you are using. Take the pan off the heat and add the tea, then leave to steep for 15 minutes. The basic proportions are 2 litres/3½ pints of water to 15g/1 tbsp loose tea leaf or about 3–5 tea bags – some teas are very strong and some are very weak so it is difficult be exact, but in my experience this ratio works with most teas. However the better the quality of tea, the less you probably need to use.
2 When brewing is finished, remove the tea bags or strain out the loose tea.
3 Dissolve the sugar in the tea. I find it does not matter so much when this is done but it is easier to dissolve whilst the tea is warm rather than cold.
4 Let the sweet tea cool down to no warmer than 35°C/95°F. It is best to use a thermometer but generally this is no warmer than finger-warm. Next, pour the brewed sweetened tea into your fermentation container.
5 Now add some of your previous kombucha batch, about 250ml/9fl oz. Or if this is the first time you are making the kombucha, you can add about 30ml/2 tbsp raw apple cider vinegar instead. To be sure you have the right kind of apple cider vinegar, it should say 'raw' or 'unpasteurised' and 'with the mother' on the bottle. Or you could buy a commercial kombucha and use this as your 'previous batch' – you'd only need to do this once.
6 Next, carefully add the scoby to the tea. Your scoby might float or sink initially, but eventually it will float on top of the liquid and take the shape of the fermentation jar you are using. If your scoby does not float this might be a sign that your scoby is inactive or dead. (If your first scoby is very small use a smaller jar and reduce the recipe to suit. Your scoby will grow quickly.)
7 Tie a cotton cloth over the jar and fasten it with an elastic band. Do not use a lid on your kombucha as it needs a little oxygen to come in.
8 Put the brew somewhere it will not be disturbed. It likes to ferment in a warm place so room temperature is good, out of direct sunlight.
9 Now, kombucha professionals say you should ferment your brew for 21 days to get all the amazing health benefits it can offer. However, I find it sometimes takes much less time. Start tasting the brew after 5–7 days; if it is too sweet for you, then ferment it for a bit longer. Personally my kombucha is normally done between 2–3 weeks but if you find it is good after 1 week then that's fine too. Some brewers will take the scoby out after a few days and let the brew continue to ferment without it. I keep the scoby in for the duration of the first fermentation.
10 When your kombucha is ready, take out the scoby, together with 250ml/9fl oz of the liquid to keep and use in your next batch.
11 You can now choose to do a second fermentation. How to do this is explained in the next recipe. This is done without the scoby and involves adding fruits or berries or fruit juice to the kombucha and then letting it ferment for a few more days to add sweetness, flavours and fizz.

GEYER
1895

Raspberry and Apricot Kombucha

Raspberries works beautifully in kombucha and apricot adds an intriguing almost vanilla-like hint. This recipe describes the second fermentation during which your kombucha will become more fizzy and take on the sweetness and flavour of the added fruits. Perhaps unexpectedly I find frozen raspberries work better than fresh, and they are available all year round! This is the kombucha second-fermentation recipe that I make the most.

1-LITRE/1¾-PINT JAR

1 litre/1¾ pints of simple kombucha (see basic recipe on page 142)

200g/7oz raspberries

8 dried sulphur-free apricots

a few fresh mint leaves to serve (optional)

1 Make the simple kombucha as described on page 142. Pour into a clean jar with a flip-top lid.
2 In a bowl, mush or blend the raspberries a little to a jam-like consistency. Chop the apricots and then add both the fruits to the kombucha.
3 Put the lid on, making sure it is 100% air-sealed so that gases stay inside the jar.
4 Let it ferment undisturbed for 24–48 hours. Test it, and if the taste and carbonation are to your liking, it is ready. Otherwise leave for another 12–24 hours.
5 Open the jar, take out the fruity bits and decant the kombucha into glass bottles. These bottles should have lids, though it does not matter what kind, screw or flip-top. The kombucha will have a lovely red colour to it now.
6 Store the bottles in the fridge; they will keep unopened for 2 months. Be careful when opening the bottles as the kombucha might be very fizzy.
7 If you find your kombucha a bit strong it can be diluted with sparkling water when serving. A sprig of fresh mint is a lovely addition.

Grapefruit, Orange and Thyme Kombucha

750ml/1¼ pints of simple kombucha (see basic recipe on page 142)

150ml/5¼fl oz freshly squeezed pink grapefruit juice

100ml/3½fl oz freshly squeezed orange juice

1–2 twigs of fresh or dried thyme

Grapefruit is another amazing flavour in kombucha. I combine it with fresh orange juice for a citrussy double-act. It is best to make your own juice for this recipe by squeezing the fruits or using a citrus juice press. Any fresh herb can be used to flavour this kombucha; rosemary is a lovely alternative to the thyme.

1-LITRE/1¾-PINT JAR

1 Make the simple kombucha as described on page 142. Pour into a clean kilner-style glass bottle with a flip-off lid and a rubber ring that seals tightly when closed.
2 Pour in the freshly squeezed juices.
3 Add the whole thyme twigs to the bottle and close the lid, making sure it seals tightly. If it isn't well sealed it will not be as fizzy. Turn the bottle upside-down carefully just once to mix.
4 Let it ferment at room temperature undisturbed for 24–48 hours. Check if it is ready by carefully opening the lid to see how fizzy it is. If not fizzy enough, ferment for another 12–24 hours.
5 Store the bottle in the fridge when finished, but remember it will continue to ferment a little so if you are planning to store it for some time it would be better to put it in the fridge even earlier on in the fermentation process.
6 Enjoy a glass decorated with a fresh slice of grapefruit and a new small twig of thyme. If you find your kombucha a bit strong just dilute it with sparkling water.

Apple and Elderflower Kombucha

Springtime is full of flowering elderflower trees, and this lovely scented flower is often used of course for elderflower lemonade and cordial, but is also amazing in fermented drinks. It has a strong flavour and it helps create lots of carbonation. Other flowers can also be used in fermentation, like rose and lavender. The apple juice is best homemade but you can also buy good-quality cold-pressed and unpasteurised apple juice if you prefer.

1-LITRE/1¾-PINT JAR

750ml/1¼ pints simple kombucha (see basic recipe on page 142)

250ml/9fl oz cold-pressed apple juice

2–3 whole heads of elderflowers

1 Make the simple kombucha as described on page 142. Pour into a clean kilner-style glass bottle with a flip-on lid that seals tightly when closed.
2 Add the fresh apple juice, leaving a 5cm/2in gap for carbonation to take place.
3 Add the elderflower heads to the bottle and close the lid, making sure it seals tightly. If it doesn't the drink will not be as fizzy as it could. Turn the bottle carefully upside-down to mix.
4 Let it ferment at room temperature undisturbed for 24–48 hours. Open the bottle to see if the taste and carbonation are to your liking. Otherwise leave for another 12–24 hours.
5 Store the bottle in the fridge when finished and remember it will continue to ferment, so if you are planning to store it for some time it's better to put it straight in the fridge without fermenting it first at room temperature.
6 If you find your kombucha a bit strong dilute it with sparkling water.

BASICS: Water Kefir

Kefir is made from a sweet carbohydrate-rich liquid using a specific water kefir culture to ferment it. This is another symbiotic culture of bacteria and yeast, but it looks nothing like a kombucha scoby and more like translucent little grains. This drink can be made from sugary water but also from other sweet liquids like fruit juices, vegetable juices, coconut water and various nut milks. Any carbohydrate sweetener can be used – sugar, coconut sugar, demerara sugar, maple syrup, honey, and agave syrup. However, sweeteners such as stevia or xylitol will not work for this (nor for any fermentation).

Water kefir should not be confused with dairy kefir. Although they are both referred to as kefir, they are two completely different types of fermentation. Dairy kefir only ferments dairy, and needs dairy to feed on – without it these kefir grains will eventually die. Water kefir does not need dairy to feed on, and feeds on any sugary liquid. The starters are both called grains because they both look like grains, however dairy kefir grains look like little cauliflower bits whilst water kefir grains are translucent.

Below: Water kefir grains are the main ingredient. Kefir grains are transparent in colour and look very much like grains, hence the name. They grow quickly and do not like to be stored too long, so need using or sharing.

This probiotic-rich drink is another staple drink in our house. We drink more of it than kombucha now but it took me a while to get into it, as it is more time-consuming to make than kombucha. You need to get into a bit of a rhythm to set off a new batch every other day or so. If you are not able to do this I might suggest you make the other drinks in this book instead and do this when you have more spare time. The fermentation process is very quick, though, taking between 24–48 hours. What I like about it is that you can get the grain to eat up all the sugar and the drink will still be delicious. With kombucha I find you do need to leave a tiny bit of sugar in for it not to taste like vinegar.

Water kefir does not last long in our fridge. It is much lighter to drink than kombucha but what is good is that you can decide for yourself how sweet you want the kefir water to be. I usually make two versions, one unsweetened one for me and one that is a little sweeter for my children. Although we do not have soft drinks or cordials in our house my children still prefer their water kefir a little bit sweet, I think to disguise the slightly bitter taste it can sometimes take on.

Water kefir grains. You must have these to be able to make water kefir. You cannot make your own grains; just as with the kombucha scoby you need to either buy or be given them from someone already making their own. The kefir grains are very sensitive, and it is easy to kill them accidentally. They like mineral-rich liquids so adding something like molasses, bicarbonate of soda (baking soda in the USA), sea salt or similar with the sugar will help keep the grains healthy.

I find that adding some fresh fruit to the liquid is good for the grains and the fermentation process. Some water kefir makers swear by ginger for the grains, as well as using less-refined sugars. Lately I have been using fresh turmeric and I have noticed the grains really like that.

The main causes of the grains dying are leaving them for too long in the fermented liquid so they get pickled, or leaving them in the fridge or freezer without using them for too long. Water kefir grains grow incredibly fast and you can almost see them expand before your eyes. Give away excess grains to all your friends and get them to brew kefir water so that you can get grains from each other if you accidently kill your own. Now and then weigh your grains and take away excess weight of grains for the amount of water you are using. It is fine to use more grains than the recipe is calling for, but not necessary.

It is good to get into a flow of making water kefir. This means that every time your water kefir is ready and fermented you should start your new batch immediately. I have got into a routine of transferring the sieved grains straight away into another batch of sugar water and starting the next ferment. If for some reason you need a break, like when you go away or are too busy, you can try and store your water kefir grains in a glass jar in your fridge without any liquid. They may not last long like this as they are very sensitive. Try not to leave them for more than a couple of weeks. You can try and freeze them; for me personally, freezing works sometimes but not always.

To stop accidentally killing the grains during brewing I have learned to never leave them for more than 48 hours. In the winter you could perhaps get away with 72 hours. After 48 hours I will separate the grains from the liquid even though it might still taste sweet. What I do then is transfer the liquid without the grains to a bottle with a tight flip-on lid and leave it out at room temperature for another 24–48 hours. This way the rest of the sugar will turn into fizz and the sugar will disappear. I used to kill my water kefir grains regularly until I started with this practice.

I haven't heard of any use of excess kefir grains, like with the kombucha scoby. If your friends don't want any spare grains from you then you might have to throw them in the compost bin. You could eat them, perhaps, although it is not something I regularly do myself.

Above: White or golden sugar makes a lighter kefir (as shown on page 155) and molasses a deeper coloured one (see page 236). Make sure the sugar is completely dissolved and not sticking to the bottom of your jar before you add the kefir grains.

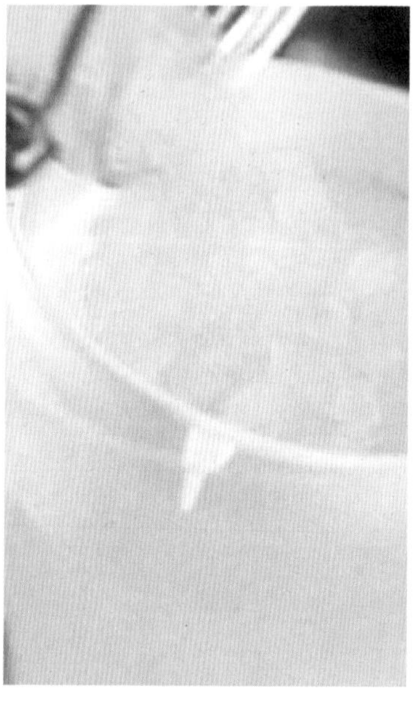

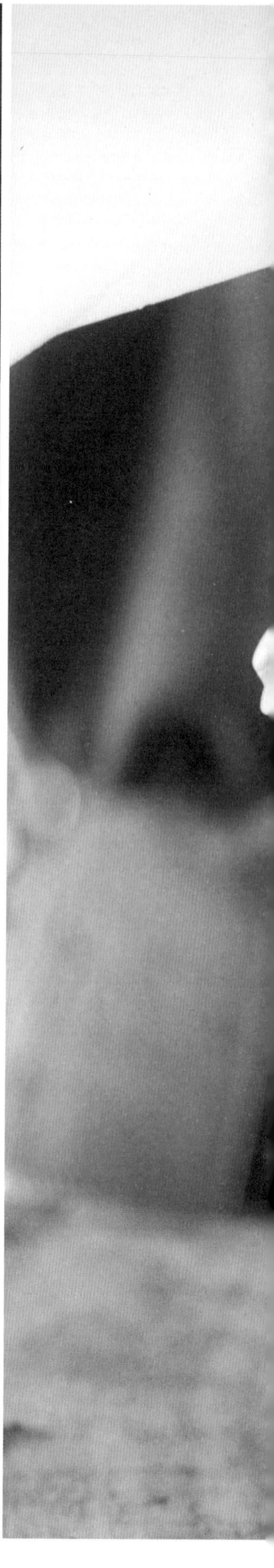

Sugary solution. As mentioned, any sugar solution will work. The grains eat any kind of carbohydrate-rich liquid. The simple first recipe I give uses sugar dissolved in water and then I go on to recipes using freshly squeezed juice. As long as there is some kind of sugar in the liquid it will work, although the more sugar you add the slightly longer it will take to ferment. The sugary water takes 48 hours to ferment but juices, coconut water and nut milks take only 24 hours.

If you are making water kefir using sugar dissolved in water, you might prefer to use a natural sugar high in minerals rather than a white sugar that has been stripped of its minerals. The darker the sugar, the more the grains will like it. So in contrast to kombucha, you can use a less-refined sugar for your water kefir. You can use coconut sugar, demerara (raw) sugar, agave syrup and maple syrup as well as white sugar. Different sugars gives different flavours to your water kefir; white sugar has the mildest flavour.

Fruits. You might like to add fruits, berries or herbs in your recipe. I recommend not adding berries with lots of seeds, like raspberries, as they will integrate with the grains and it is difficult to separate and remove them. Also mushy fruits like bananas or ripe pears are not great as they will also be difficult to get out of the grains later.

Water. Filtered tap water or bottled still spring water is best. You do need to filter the water to remove the chlorine, as this disturbs the fermentation process. See page 30 for more information.

Fermentation jar. This can be any shape and size, just make sure it is clean. Use either glass, ceramic or clay, but not plastic as chemicals can leach, and not metals, as these can corrode. Whereas with kombucha it is important to let oxygen flow in during the fermentation process and therefore important not to use a tight-fitting lid, with water kefir it does not matter. You can use a jar with a lid, or one without a lid and a muslin cotton cloth to cover instead. Personally, I like to use a kilner-style glass jar with a clip-on lid and keep the lid on for the duration of the fermentation process.

Plastic sieve and wooden spoon. A sieve is used to strain the liquid from the grains. Don't use metal sieves as the grains are very sensitive. Similarly, use wooden not metal spoons when touching the kefir grains.

Left: These pictures summarise the simple sequence of water kefir making. The sugar is added to the measured water and allowed to dissolve, stirring occasionally if needed. The kefir water grains are added, and gently stirred with a non-metal utensil. The lid is sealed, and the kefir is left to ferment in a suitable location. When ready, a plastic sieve or strainer is used to separate the grains from the water into a separate clean jug or pitcher. (The grains can then be used to start off another batch of water.) The kefir liquid is poured into a flip-top bottle. This bottle can be left at room temperature to continue to ferment slightly, in order to remove the last bit of sugar and to make it more fizzy, or you can put it directly into the fridge to chill, ready to enjoy. Keep an eye on fermenting bottles; you don't want them to explode.

Simple Lemon Water Kefir

This is a good recipe to start with, and I suggest you follow it until your grains start to grow, which they will do very quickly if done properly without any breaks. When they start to multiply you can start to experiment with other recipes and have several on the go. And then you will always have some extra grains in case you accidentally kill some of them.

When you make sugar water kefir, it helps to add some fruit to it. It will ferment better, and will take on the flavour you put in the water. In this recipe I use lemon, but you can choose other fruits.

I often like to add molasses, about 5ml/1 tsp, for its mineral content, and to use coconut sugar; this makes a darker-looking kefir, as pictured on page 236. I sometimes also add a little sea salt or bicarbonate of soda.

1.5-LITRE/2½-PINT JAR

75g/2½oz organic golden sugar
1 litre/1¾ pints filtered water
½ organic unwaxed lemon
2cm/5in fresh ginger root
100g/3½oz water kefir grains

1 Dissolve the sugar in the filtered water; this is easier if you warm it up slightly, but allow the liquid to then cool down before using.
2 Slice the lemon into thin slices. Keep the peel on if unwaxed but take it off if waxed. Slice the ginger.
3 Add the water kefir grains to your clean glass or ceramic fermentation jar. If you have a previous batch of kefir you could add 100ml/3½fl oz of this, but it is not necessary.
4 Carefully pour the cooled-down sweet water over your kefir grains in the fermentation jar. Add the lemon and the ginger slices. Put the lid on or use a cotton cloth to cover and secure it with an elastic band.
5 Ferment untouched at room temperature for 24–48 hours.
6 When done, strain out the lemon and ginger (use a plastic sieve over a clean glass jug; the grains can then go straight into your next batch of kefir water that you have prepared ready, the routine of a good kefir maker).
7 Transfer the fermented water kefir to a glass bottle and seal tightly with a lid – any type of lid here is fine. Leave out for another day or two for carbonation to happen.
8 When happy with the level of carbonation, you can store in the fridge. Water kefir, just like kombucha, will continue to ferment slightly in the fridge but can be stored for several months. Be careful when opening a stored water kefir as it can be very fizzy.
9 You can do a second fermentation if you like. I normally just add a few bits of fruit for a second fermentation, as the kefir water is already flavoured with lemon and ginger from the first. I strain out the grains using a plastic sieve, then pour the kefir water into 1-litre/1¾-pint bottles, leaving a little space to add a few raspberries, a small handful of raisins, or goji berries. Then I secure the lids and leave at room temperature for another 24–48 hours. (Do not forget your bottles as they can explode if there is too much pressure. This has never happened to me, but it has to several of my students.) I then transfer the bottles to the fridge without taking out the fruits, and let it get really cool before drinking. When you open they can be fizzy, so take care.

Apple and Beetroot Juice Kefir

A fresh vegetable juice or fruit juice is another sweet liquid you can add your kefir grains to. You can use any juice for this recipe but apple and beetroot is a particularly lovely combination. Adding kefir grains and fermenting for 24 hours adds a slight fizz to the sweetness; you will still have all the benefits of the apple and beetroot, and with added probiotic strains it becomes a super-healthy juice. Note that your kefir grains will become and stay pink for some time after making this ferment!

You can use bought or homemade juice but it is nicer to make your own if you have a juicer. Use a third of beetroots and two-thirds of apples until you have a litre of it. Many health food shops have a juice bar and will make up juices exactly how you want them or you can buy them separately as apple juice and beet juice and then mix them yourself.

1.5-LITRE/2½-PINT JAR

1 litre/1¾ pints cold-pressed unpasteurised apple and beetroot juice
100g/3½oz water kefir grains

1 Pour the apple and beetroot juice into the clean jar, I use a glass kilner-style jar with a flip-off lid.
2 Add the water kefir grains.
3 Ferment for 24–48 hours, probably closer to 24 than 48 hours. This ferment is quicker than with the sugary water.
4 When the kefir drink is ready, transfer to glass bottles and store in the fridge. It will usually keep a couple of weeks in the fridge, but it is better to drink straight away. Be careful when opening it if you choose to store it, as it can get fizzy.

For more guidance see the simple kefir recipe instructions on page 154.

Elderflower and Lemon Kefir

When elderflowers are in season I use the gorgeous flowers in every single ferment I can – they work amazingly well with the kefir grains and I love their taste. Elderflowers are great for your immune system and a remedy for allergies, colds, flus and respiratory disturbances. This kefir may also lower blood sugar levels and be good for constipation!

1.5-LITRE/2½-PINT JAR

1 litre/1¾ pints filtered water
75g/2½oz organic golden sugar
½ organic unwaxed lemon
4 whole heads of elderflowers
100g/3½oz water kefir grains

1 Dissolve the sugar in the water; this is easiest if you warm it up slightly, but make sure you cool the liquid down before using.
2 Slice the lemon into thin slices. Keep the peel on if unwaxed but take it off if waxed.
3 Make sure there is no dirt or insects on the flowers but try not to wash them.
4 Add your grains to your glass or ceramic fermentation jar. If you have a previous batch of kefir you could add 100ml/3½fl oz, but it is not necessary.
5 Carefully pour the cooled-down sweet water over the kefir grains. Add the lemon slices and the elderflower heads, making sure the elderflowers are underneath the surface. Put the lid on or use a muslin cotton cloth to cover and secure with an elastic band.
6 Ferment at room temperature for 48 hours.
7 When done, remove the lemon and flowers and strain the liquid from the grains with a plastic sieve. (You can put the grains into a new batch of kefir and start the next fermentation process.)
8 Transfer the strained liquid to smaller glass bottles, seal with tight-fitting lids, and leave out for another day or two for carbonation to happen.
9 When happy with how fizzy it is, you can transfer to the fridge. Water kefir, just like kombucha, will continue to ferment slightly in the fridge but can be stored for several months. Be careful when opening a stored water kefir as it can be very fizzy. A slice or few of fresh lemon is nice to serve in a glass of the kefir.

For more guidance see the simple kefir recipe instructions on page 154.

Coconut Water Kefir

This drink contains not only all the beneficial Lactobacillus bacteria but also offers the amazing health benefits of coconut water. Coconut water contains essential minerals and electrolytes and is similar in its chemical structure to our own blood plasma. These two ingredients combined create a super-health drink indeed. This kefir would be good for digestion, kidneys and the immune system, and for protecting your heart against high blood pressure, heart attack, irregular heartbeat and blood clots. I like to drink a glass a day.

Unless you find some really sweet young coconut, this drink might not taste quite as nice as it is healthy. If you don't like it, you could use it as a base for a smoothie or do a second fermentation. This drink is a true elixir of life.

You can also make a coconut milk kefir, which tastes very different – this is in the fermented nut-dairy chapter, on page 215.

1.5-LITRE/2½-PINT JAR

1 litre/1¾ pints coconut water, from fresh young coconuts, or if you can't get hold of these use bought coconut water

few slices of fresh ginger or lemon (optional)

75g/2½oz water kefir grains

1 Open the coconuts and strain the water from any bits from the shell. Or, use a bottle of bought coconut water. Pour the liquid into your clean fermentation jar.
2 Slice the ginger and/or lemon if using, and add to the liquid.
3 Add the water kefir grains to the liquid in the jar.
4 Leave to ferment for 24–36 hours at room temperature. This drink is nicer-tasting if it is fermented for a shorter rather than longer time, but again this does depends on how warm the temperature is in your room. I normally decant after 24 hours rather than 36 hours, but somewhere in-between might be the best.
5 Strain the grains for the next batch, using a plastic sieve.
6 Transfer the fermented coconut liquid to a bottle with a lid, and put in the fridge to cool. Drink up soon, but this drink will store for a couple of weeks in the fridge.

For more guidance see the simple kefir recipe instructions on page 154.

Rejuvelac

This fermented drink is made from the soak water of sprouted wheat berries and other grains. There are two stages: you need to sprout the grains and then you need to ferment them in water. It is a brilliant digestive tonic, and is a lovely drink to have especially after a second fermentation but it is also great to use as a starter in other fermented drinks and foods. You can use any kind of grain to do this drink or a mixture of them – I have made successful rejuvelac from wheat, spelt, kamut, rye and quinoa.

300g/10½oz wheat berries
2 litres/3½ pints filtered water (as well as water for soaking)

2-LITRE/3½-PINT JAR

1 Firstly soak the wheat berries covered completely in filtered water for 8 hours.
2 Drain and rinse the grains and put them in a sprouting jar or a glass. If you use a glass jar, cover the opening with a cotton cloth and secure with a rubber band. Then, position it almost upside down at a 45-degree angle so that water can get out but the grains will still be moist and not dry out. If you use a sprouting jar just follow the manufacturer's instructions for your specific jar.
3 Keep at room temperature and rinse the grains twice daily, discarding the rinsing water, and re-positioning the jar each time as before.
4 Continue until you can see a small small green sprout starting to grow – it looks like a little tail on the berry. When you can see little sprouts on all the berries they are ready. This takes about 2 days depending on the quality of the berry used. Rinse the sprouts again until the water runs clear.
5 Put the sprouts in a 2-litre/3½-pint glass jar and fill up with about 1.5 litres/2½ pints of filtered water. Cover the jar with a cotton or muslin cloth, securing it with an elastic band.
6 Let ferment undisturbed at room temperature for 2–3 days. When it is done you should see tiny little bubbles in a slightly yellow and cloudy drink and it should have a lemony almost liquorice-like taste from the wheat.
7 Strain the wheat berry sprouts and pour the water into glass bottles, to store in the fridge. Or you can now do a second fermentation if you want, to add other fruit flavours.
8 You can use the sprouted wheat berries for several other batches of rejuvelac without having to sprout new ones. This time you can add some of your previous rejuvelac as a starter. You can use the sprouted berries for probably 10–20 batches of rejuvelac before you need to discard them.

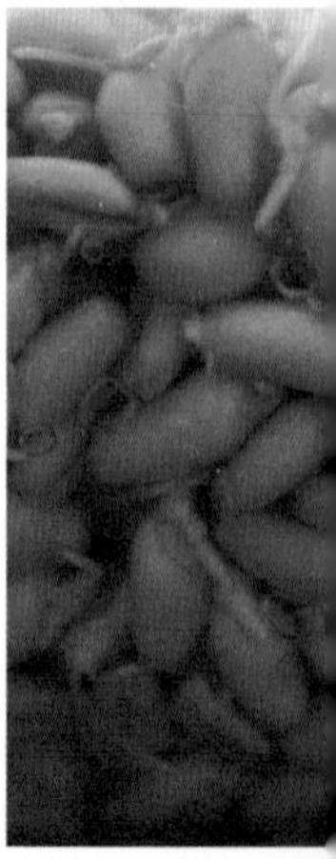

Fermented Rhubarb Fizz

Anyone with rhubarb in their allotment will know how much produce you can end up with. When you are bored with making crumble, and have a fridge full of fermented rhubarbs, this is a great way of using the beautiful-looking vegetable. Yes, rhubarb is actually a vegetable even though we mostly make sweet things out of it.

1-LITRE/1¾-PINT JAR

700g/1½lb rhubarb
1 litre/1¾ pints filtered water
75ml/2½fl oz/5 tbsp agave syrup
45ml/3 tbsp freshly squeezed lemon juice
15g/1 tbsp sugar
15g/1 tbsp freshly grated ginger root
½ probiotic capsule (content only)

1 Rinse the rhubarb and cut up in small pieces, then put in a saucepan with the measured water.
2 Boil the rhubarb for 5 minutes or so until the pieces have started to disintegrate. Let cool to room temperature.
3 Over a large bowl to retain the liquid, strain the rhubarb through a muslin cloth or a nut milk bag. You can press down the purée if needed.
4 Add the syrup, lemon juice, sugar, ginger and probiotic to the cooled-down liquid. Stir until all dissolved.
5 Pour into clean glass bottles with a swing flip-top lid.
6 Let ferment for 2–3 days. Check after 2 days to see if there is enough carbonation for your liking; if not leave it for another day.
7 Store in the fridge when ready. Serve chilled. It will keep for a month in the fridge unopened.

Ginger Beer

Ginger beer is not very popular in Sweden where I come from so I had never really heard about it before I came to the UK, where it is a traditional soft drink loved by all ages. This is a wonderful healthy version of ginger beer. There are several ways to make it; this recipe uses a homemade ginger bug starter to help with the fermentation – you will need to make this beforehand so start the process a few days ahead. I love to also make this with turmeric, adding 30–60g/1–2oz of freshly grated root with the ginger.

2-LITRE/3½-PINT JAR

75g/2½oz fresh organic ginger root
1.5 litres/2½ pints filtered water
150g/5¼oz sugar
30ml/2 tbsp ginger bug starter (see below)

1 Wash the ginger well but do not peel it. Grate the ginger.
2 Put the ginger in a saucepan with the filtered water and bring to the boil. Let it boil for 20 minutes.
3 Strain over a bowl to retain the liquid and discard the ginger root.
4 Add the sugar to the hot water and stir to dissolve. Leave to cool down to room temperature.
5 Add the ginger bug starter to the liquid and stir well.
6 Pour the liquid into your clean fermentation jar or directly into bottles with flip-on lids, but make sure the ginger bug is equally shared between the bottles if you have more than one and leave a little space at the top for carbonation. Seal the jar or the bottles.
7 Let the ginger beer ferment for 2–3 days at room temperature.
8 After 2–3 days you will see little bubbles in the ginger beer. It is then ready, but you can check that you are happy with the level of fizz by opening the lid. If not then you can ferment for another 12–24 hours.
9 If still in the fermentation jar, pour the ginger beer into glass bottles with swing flip-top lids. Leave a 3cm/1¼in space at the tops for carbonation.
10 Transfer to the fridge where they can be stored for a month or so. Try to drink them soon, however, as they continue to ferment even in the fridge.

GINGER BUG STARTER

This bug can be used as a starter, instead of a probiotic capsule for example (see page 32). For a fermented juice, just add 30ml/2 tbsp ginger bug starter to 1 litre/1¾ pints of juice and ferment for 1–3 days.

GINGER BUG STARTER
large piece of organic fresh ginger root
250ml/9fl oz filtered water
75g/2½oz white sugar

1 Wash the ginger but you don't need to peel it if it is organic. Grate 15g/1 tbsp of the fresh piece and keep the rest for adding later.
2 Put the grated ginger in a clean 300ml/½pint glass jar with 50ml/1¾fl oz of the filtered water and 15g/1 tbsp of the sugar. Stir and cover the jar with a cotton cloth secured with an elastic band.
3 Leave at room temperature for 24 hours.
4 Repeat the process every day for 4 days, stirring in 1 tbsp of grated ginger and 1 tbsp of sugar each day.
5 On day 5 you should have a fizzy mixture and it should smell a bit yeasty. The ginger bug is then active and ready to use. Store in a sealed jar in the fridge until needed. It will keep for 3 or even more weeks in the fridge.

Traditional Bread and Beet Kvass

Kvass is best made with a starter – various types can be used, like sourdough, yeast, probiotic powder, ginger bug, or dairy whey. This recipe is for the classic kvass made from dry rye bread, with a sourdough starter or a bit of yeast. If you are a home baker you will have all the ingredients in your kitchen already. I don't personally make this a lot but it is a very pleasant and refreshing drink. If you are unable to get hold of rye bread you could try it with other stale bread you have at home, and you could use a packet of dried yeast instead of sourdough starter. This drink is often used in cooking.

2-LITRES/3½-PINT JAR

500g/1lb dry rye bread
2 litres/3½ pints filtered water
50g/1¾oz sourdough starter
50ml/1¾fl oz/3¼ tbsp agave syrup
juice of ½ lemon
small pinch of salt
1 fresh beetroot, peeled and diced

1 Cut the rye bread into 4cm/1½in squares. If they aren't dry you can roast them in a low heat in the oven for 15 minutes; 100°C/212°F should be enough.
2 Boil the measured water in a saucepan, take off the heat and add the dry bread pieces. Make sure they stay underneath the water surface. You can put a plate on top to make sure of this.
3 Cover with a cotton teacloth and let soak overnight.
4 When this is done you want the water and not the bread, so you need to strain it using a colander, a sieve or even better a nut milk bag or muslin cloth so you can squeeze the water out. Discard the bread.
5 Pour this strained water into your clean fermentation jar. This should be made from glass, ceramic, clay or stoneware. The jar does not need to have a lid.
6 Add the starter, syrup, lemon juice and salt to the jar and stir so all get dissolved. Stir in the diced beetroot.
7 Cover the jar with a cotton cloth and secure with an elastic band.
8 Let ferment at room temperature for 2–3 days. You can stir the kvass now and then if you remember.
9 Once you see the kvass is bubbling, it is ready. Strain the liquid into glass bottles with a swing flip-top lid, discarding the beetroot. Seal the lid and let ferment for another 12–24 hours.
10 Store in the fridge.

Raspberry and Pear Kvass

This is a lovely summer drink. You can use a probiotic capsule as a starter or try with ginger bug. This kvass is very refreshing.

1-LITRE/1¾-PINT JAR

200g/7oz fresh or frozen raspberries

handful of fresh mint leaves

1–2 pears

1 litre/1¾ pints filtered water

45ml/3 tbsp agave syrup

1 probiotic capsule (content only) or 30ml/2 tbsp active ginger bug starter (see page 166)

15ml/1 tbsp lemon juice

15g/1 tbsp grated fresh ginger (optional)

1 Wash the raspberries and mint if needed. If they are organic or home-grown, just make sure there are no insects or dirt. Wash the pears, peel them if non-organic, and cut into chunks.

2 Put 200ml/7fl oz of the water into your clean fermentation jar. It should be a kilner-style jar with a rubber seal and flip-off lid so it can be sealed tightly later. Add the syrup, and the probiotic powder or ginger bug starter, and stir to dissolve.

3 Add the lemon juice and the grated ginger if using, then fill up with the remaining water.

4 Make sure the lid is sealed tight. Let ferment at room temperature for 2–3 days. It should be ready when you see little bubbles in the jar.

5 When ready strain the fruit out of the liquid and pour into glass bottles with a swing flip-off lid. Seal tightly and let ferment for another 24 hours at room temperature before storing it in the fridge. It will keep a couple of weeks in the fridge but carries on fermenting slightly so be careful when you are opening the bottle. Serve chilled.

Spiced Winter Kvass

This lovely Christmassy-flavoured kvass is enjoyed by everyone in our household. It is usually served chilled but can also be gently heated to make a warm toddy. It will keep well for a month in the fridge.

5 apples
1 litre/1¾ pints filtered water
30ml/2 tbsp agave syrup
1 probiotic capsule (content only)
5g/1 tsp ground nutmeg
4cm/1½in fresh ginger, sliced
4 cloves, gently crushed
3 cinnamon sticks, slightly crushed
2 whole cardamom seeds
1 star anise, split in half

1.5-LITRE/2½-PINT JAR

1 Wash and cut the apples into 10 wedges each.
2 Pour 200ml/7fl oz of the water into your clean fermentation jar. It should be a kilner-style jar with a rubber seal and flip-off lid so it can be sealed tightly later. Add the syrup, probiotic powder and nutmeg, and allow to dissolve.
3 Add all the rest of the spices to your fermentation jar. Fill up with the remaining water.
4 Make sure the lid is on and sealed tight. Turn upside-down a couple of times to mix the kvass. Let ferment at room temperature for 2–3 days. You should see bubbles in the jar when ready.
5 When ready, strain the liquid from the fruit and spices into a glass bottle with a swing flip-off lid. Seal tightly and let ferment for another 24 hours at room temperature before storing it in the fridge.

Fermented Nordic Yulemust

This is a healthy fermented version of a fizzy soft drink we typically have at Christmas in Sweden. My aunty posted me this recipe and I got really excited as the drink is not that easy to get hold of outside Sweden unless you live close to IKEA – it is absolutely delicious and definitely tastes similar to the original version although not as sweet, which is a good thing. When I give this drink to non-Swedes they usually say they have never tried anything like it but they think the most similar thing would be a root beer crossed with cola. You will have to be the judge of it when you make it.

2.5-LITRE/4½-PINT JAR

350g/12½oz dark sugar, such as muscovado or demerara

100g/3½oz raisins

4 dried figs

3 prunes

75g/2½oz fresh ginger root, grated

75g/2½oz dried juniper berries

10 green cardamom pods, slightly crushed

5 whole cinnamon sticks

4 cloves

2 pieces of dried bitter orange peel

2 dried mace (this is the covering of a nutmeg)

1 star anise

5g/1tsp coriander seeds

2 litres/3½ pints filtered water

zest and juice of 1 lemon

zest and juice of 1 orange

150ml/5¼fl oz active ginger bug starter (see page 166)

1 Put all the ingredients apart from lemon juice, orange juice and ginger bug starter in a pan with 1 litre/1¾ pints of the water. Bring to the boil and let simmer for 20 minutes.

2 Take off the heat and pour in the other litre of water. Also add the lemon juice and orange juice. Cover with cling film or plastic wrap, and let steep for 24 hours.

3 Then strain out the spices, retaining the liquid. Mix in the ginger bug starter and stir carefully.

4 Pour into a clean kilner-style or mason jar with a flip-top lid and a rubber seal. Close the lid tightly and let ferment undisturbed for 2–3 days.

5 Open up to taste it. You can add more sweetener if you want to, or some more orange juice, depending on what you think might be missing.

6 When you are happy with the taste, pour the liquid into bottles with a tight-fitting lid so no gases can escape. Leave at room temperature to ferment for another 24 hours.

7 When ready, store in the fridge. Drink within a few weeks.

CHAPTER SEVEN:
Fermented Dairy

In this chapter I cover dairy kefir, yogurt, whey and strained yogurt (or labneh). In Scandinavia, where I am from, we eat a lot of fermented dairy. The fridges in the supermarkets are literally packed with different kinds of dairy products, many of which are only known in the Nordic countries, such as fil, long-fil, ymer, kvark, and skyr. Dairy is a staple in Scandinavia, and you will find it as an ingredient in many foods (it is not an easy part of the world to be dairy-free or lactose-intolerant in). I am going to cover just a few, very easy to make, fermented dairy recipes in this chapter. If you find them exciting, there are many other different dairy ferments you can explore outside of this book.

Dairy is not tolerated by all and is a source of allergies and sensitivities for many of my clients. Some people, and it is more common in Asian countries, lack the specific enzymes that break down dairy which leave them unable to digest dairy at all, often without realising, which can be a cause of years of unecessary suffering. I also have many vegan or plant-based clients. However, for those able or willing, dairy can be an amazingly nutritious food, full of protein, healthy fats and minerals. Fermented dairy is much easier for us to digest than non-fermented dairy and much better tolerated by most people, and it is my preferred way to eat dairy produce if you choose to do so.

We have been advised by some holistic health advisers to avoid dairy, but milk kefir is now hugely popular – it is, counterintuitively, even said to cure dairy intolerances. There has been research into fermented dairy kefir that does indeed indicate it is good for our gut. Because of the fat and the protein, it seems we can integrate the beneficial bacteria in a more efficient way than from ferments that do not contain fat and protein. If we are to trust research, the health benefits already discussed can all be achieved by regularly eating dairy kefir. And apart from proteins and healthy fats your dairy kefir also contains magnesium, calcium, biotin, folic acid, vitamin K2, vitamin A, vitamin D and plenty of probiotics. The recipes in this chapter can be made with cow's, goat's or ewe's milk.

BASICS: Milk Kefir

I am starting this chapter with dairy kefir. This has been hailed by some as almost a magic potion for well-being because of its probiotic effect in our gut. It is very easy and satisfying to make milk kefir. The result is a liquid thicker than milk, but thinner than yogurt. Kefir has a sour taste, like yogurt, but you can do a second fermentation if you wish to add some sweetness and flavour to it.

Milk kefir can be enjoyed as it is with your cereal or granola instead of ordinary milk. I also often use it in smoothie recipes for an extra bit of protein and probiotics. For good probiotic effect you could have a small glass in the morning on an empty stomach. You can use kefir in any recipe to replace milk, for example in pancakes, sauces and dips, and in your baking recipes. If you are vegan you can get the same health benefits from coconut milk kefir (see page 215).

Dairy kefir grains. The culture used are milk kefir grains, which are different to water kefir grains. These grains have a white and rubbery texture, looking a little like cauliflower florets. The grains are made from beneficial bacteria and yeast and they will multiply with time and can be

dehydrated for long-term storage. If looked after properly your dairy kefir grains will last indefinitely. If you aren't using the grains for a while, you can store them in the fridge in a little milk that you can replace now and then.

The milk kefir grains need to be active to ferment. If you get dehydrated grains you must activate them by soaking them in a little bit of milk for 7 days, changing the milk daily and discarding the used milk. The grains should be white and cauliflower-looking when done, and only then are the grains active. You can also get dried kefir powder; this can only be used once i.e. for one batch, and does not grow as with the normal grains.

Dairy milk. You can make kefir from cow's, goat's and ewe's milk. Both pasteurised and raw milk can be used, however the chosen milk should be organic and preferably full-fat or whole. The nutritional content is higher, and it is worth noting that this is even more so for goat's milk than for cow's. Always choose to buy dairy from organic farms and from animals that can roam freely, grazing in green pastures.

Fruits. You might like to add fruits, berries or herbs in a second fermentation.

Fermentation jar. This can be any shape and size, just make sure it is scrupulously clean. You can use one with a lid, or one without a lid and a muslin cotton cloth to cover instead. Oxygen can come into the jar, or not. If you use a lid you need to burp it daily or, preferably, use a special fermentation lid as discussed on page 36, as this dairy ferment can actually explode quite easily. It has happened with me twice! Do not use metal or plastic jars; glass or ceramic are best.

Kefir professionals argue that the fermentation jar should not be washed in between batches, and that this will help with the fermentation process and make an even better kefir. Personally, I do wash it but not every time. Perhaps every 5 times... it's up to you. I have noticed that if you wash the jar the next batch will take slightly longer to ferment.

Plastic sieve. This is used to strain the liquid from the grains. Don't use metal sieves as the grains are very sensitive. Similarly, use wooden not metal spoons when touching the grains.

Left: These pictures summarise the simple sequence of dairy kefir making. The grains are added to the milk, and gently stirred with a non-metal utensil. The special fermentation lid is sealed, and the kefir is left to ferment in a suitable location. When ready, a plastic sieve or strainer is used to separate the grains from the liquid into a clean jug or pitcher. (The grains can then be used to start off another batch.) The milk kefir is poured into a bottle, ready to chill or to use in a second fermentation.

Simple Milk Kefir

This is a good recipe to start with, and I suggest you follow it until your grains start to grow, which they will do very quickly if done properly without any breaks.

Dairy kefir has a very sour taste after the first fermentation, that does not appeal to everyone. A second fermentation (described overleaf) will help with mellowing the sour flavour and I also sometimes add a few drops of stevia when I drink or eat it, which will neutralise the sourness. Stevia is a natural sweetener made from the stevia herb.

1 litre/1¾ pints organic full-fat (whole) milk
45g/3 tbsp active milk kefir grains

1-LITRE/1¾-PINT JAR

1 Pour the milk into your clean fermentation jar. This can be a jar with or without a lid.
2 Add the milk kefir grains and shake lightly or stir so they mix.
3 Either put the lid on or use a cotton cloth to cover and secure with an elastic band. If you are using a lid, you must be sure to open the lid once a day to let the gases out or get a proper fermentation lid with an airlock. You don't want to forget to burp it and risk an exploding jar.
4 Let ferment at room temperature for 24–48 hours (longer in the winter, when it is colder). You can shake it now and then if you remember.
5 Once fermented, strain out the kefir grains using a plastic or nylon sieve as the grains are sensitive to metal. Keep the grains for their next use; you don’t need to rinse them.
6 Pour the fermented kefir into glass bottles. You can put these straight into the fridge if you prefer, as it is now ready to drink. However it is also good to sit at room temperature without the grains for another 24–48 hours as this will thicken the kefir as well as making it less sour and more creamy – or you can do this second fermentation stage with added fruit, as described in the following recipe.
7 Kefir can be stored for several months in the fridge if unopened. Transfer the grains into a fresh batch of milk and start the process again.

Berry Kefir

After you have made your simple milk kefir and taken out the grains, you can choose to do a second fermentation. This will make your kefir creamier and less sour.

For a second fermentation you simply pour the ready-made kefir into a clean glass bottle without the grains, and leave it to ferment at room temperature for another 24–48 hours. You can choose to add nothing to your kefir at this stage or you can add fruits, berries or spices as described below. This will add delicious flavour and sweetness to your kefir.

batch of simple milk kefir, see page 185 (with grains strained and removed)

100g/3½oz frozen mixed berries (raspberries, blueberries, blackberries, etc.)

1 Add the kefir and berries to a clean glass bottle with a fermentation lid. Shake or turn the bottle to mix the ingredients.

2 Let ferment at room temperature for 12–48 hours, depending on how warm it is in your room. If not using a special fermentation jar, you must remember to open the lid briefly to burp the ferment once a day.

3 When done, you can either leave the berries in the kefir or strain them out. If you are planning to store the kefir for longer than a week it is better to strain the berries out. You can store your ready-made kefir in any glass bottle or jar now.

4 Keep in the fridge. If unopened the kefir should last for several months.

Homemade Yogurt

Yogurt is more commonly eaten than kefir, but making it is not quite as easy. It is nonetheless well worth a try. There are many ways to make yogurt, but all you need is milk, a starter, and then some kind of incubator that will warm your milk at a constant level. A food thermometer is also highly recommended.

The choice of milk is important as this will make a difference to the end result. Just as with kefir, you should choose an organic full-fat milk as it always turns out nicer, and the nutritional profile is better. You can use raw milk if you can find it but pasteurised also works well. You can use cow's, goat's or ewe's milk.

The starter can either be a store-bought yogurt starter, or better still and cheaper, you can use a commercially-produced yogurt. After your first time you can of course just use some of your previous batch of homemade yogurt. If you choose a store-bought yogurt as your starter, make sure it is made from fresh milk and not from milk powder and that it has a live culture inside.

The incubator can be one of many kitchen items. I use my dehydrator or crockpot to make yogurt but you can also use a heating pad, your oven or a yogurt maker.

300-ML/½-PINT JAR

1 litre/1¾ pints organic full-fat (whole) milk
30ml/2 tbsp previously-made yogurt or bought bio-live yogurt

1 Warm the milk in a stainless steel pan to 80–90°C/176–194°F, stirring it well and then letting it cool to 45°C/113°F. This heating stage changes the structure of the protein in the milk, making it set to a more solid form of yogurt. You could however get away with not doing this step if you don't mind your yogurt separating slightly.
2 When the milk has cooled to 45°C/113°F, add the 2 tablespoons of your starter yogurt, stirring it very carefully just enough to incorporate it fully into the milk.
3 Pour the yogurt into clean glass jars of your choice.
4 Now, put the glass jars into the incubator to provide a constant heat of around 42–45°C/107–113°F. The jars should stay here for 12–24 hours. If you do not have an incubator or yogurt maker, you can try doing it in your oven with only the light on, which should heat the oven up very slightly; in some well-insulated ovens it will reach around 42°C/107°F.
5 After 12–24 hours you can put the jars into the fridge and let them set properly. If you find your yogurt too loose in consistency you can strain it through a cheesecloth or nut milk bag to get a thicker result, if you want.
6 Enjoy your yogurt, which should keep for several weeks stored covered in the fridge.

Dairy Whey

Whey is basically the liquid part of milk. It is what remains after the milk has been curdled and strained, and is a by-product of cheese-making. Homemade whey can be used as a starter in any fermentation recipe. In Europe it is not used in much else than in other fermented dairy, but in American recipes, you will see whey even in fermented vegetable recipes. I don't use whey myself as I personally think it gives a sour milk taste to the fermented vegetables. However, many people like to use this as a starter as it can work very well (it is in the chart on page 32), so therefore I wanted to include it in the book.

Whey comes from milk, but we make it from bio-live yogurt. The curds left in the cloth aren't wasted, of course, they can be used to make labneh, a delicious soft fermented cheese, given overleaf.

To strain, you will need either a cheesecloth, a muslin cloth, a nut milk bag or a coffee filter. A coffee filter is the easiest if you have a holder for it, but you might have to do the yogurt in two batches. If you have a filter coffee machine you can use this for the whole process, using the coffee pot as your bowl that catches the whey.

500ml/17½fl oz organic full-fat plain (whole) bio-live yogurt; your own homemade one would be good (see page 188)

1 Pour the yogurt into your muslin bag or other strainer, letting it strain for 8 hours or overnight to allow all the liquid or whey drip through. Do not force or press this dripping of liquid. You want the liquid as clear as possible.
2 When the dripping has stopped, pour the whey into a clean glass jar and keep it in the fridge until used. It can be stored for 2 months in the fridge.

Fresh Chive and Fennel Labneh

What is left in the muslin after whey-making on the previous page is not going to get wasted. It makes a wonderful base for a fresh cream cheese, or labneh as it is also called. You will of course use your newly made yogurt curds as the base but if you want a really creamy labneh you should start with a thick Greek-style strained yogurt with a high fat content. My mother used to make this for our Friday cosy nights when I was a child; we used to finish the whole lot in one night.

The strained yogurt left over from making whey will have a fairly thick consistency, so thick that you can make little cheese balls out of it and roll in some dried herbs. Labneh will keep for several weeks in the fridge if untouched but usually gets eaten up straightaway.

batch of strained curds from bio-live yogurt (a by-product of the whey recipe on page 190)

1 garlic clove, minced

small bunch of fresh chives, finely chopped

15g/1 tbsp finely diced fennel (bulb and leaves)

2.5g/½ tsp salt

1 Add the herbs and salt to the yogurt in a bowl, and mix well. You might want to adjust the measurements to your own taste. Store in a clean container in the fridge. That's it!

CHAPTER EIGHT:

Fermented Nut Dairy

In this chapter, I will go through how to use nuts and seeds to make dairy-free yogurt, cheese and kefir products. I am especially excited about the nut cheeses as these are such an excellent alternative to normal cheese if you are trying to avoid dairy. I would not go as far as to say that nut cheese tastes quite the same as dairy cheese but it is definitely similar.

Nuts are a great way of getting healthy fats, protein and minerals into your diet. There is a lot of evidence-based research indicating that nuts are good for health and longevity. Research also tells us nuts do not make you fat, which is sometimes a concern.

However, nuts and seeds can be hard for some people to digest. They do contain lots of enzyme inhibitors and anti-nutrients. Sprouting and fermenting nuts will help them become more digestible as well as increasing the nutrient content tremendously. Nuts cannot be sprouted, but they can be activated, which is the equivalent to sprouting seeds and grains. If nuts are soaked it makes it much easier for us to digest them and assimilate their nutrients. Fermenting makes the digestion even easier.

The best nuts to use in nut cheesemaking are cashews, almonds and macadamia nuts. These are good because they do not have skins, or it is easy to get rid of the skins. You can make cheese from other nuts as well, but the skins can make your nut cheese less appealing in colour and also taste slightly bitter. You can, however, swap any nut in these recipes for another of your choice.

You can also make the recipes with seeds, although you should be aware that these have a more distinctive flavour and can turn bitter and darker in colour after fermentation; a good alternative can be to use about 50% nuts and 50% seeds.

The picture opposite shows nut cheeses of various maturations, left natural or rolled in paprika powder, or dried herbs. In the chapter I have also included a delicious fermented chocolate nut 'cheesecake', and you can easily adapt the recipe to make a lemon and lime cheesecake. If you are avoiding dairy for one reason or another, this chapter is an introduction to an exciting new world of plant-based wholefood.

Fermented Cashew Nut Cheese

Cashews are good nuts to ferment as there is no skin on them, they have a neutral flavour, and aren't too expensive compared to many other skinless nuts (although to be accurate, cashews are in fact a seed rather than a nut). You are also able to get a completely smooth consistency with cashews, like cream, which makes a lovely texture.

This is a soft, quite spreadable cheese. A grinding of black pepper is a nice seasoning. You can press it and mature it for a harder texture and stronger taste, as described overleaf.

250g/9oz cashew nuts
pinch of fine salt
2.5g/½ tsp coconut sugar powder (optional)
75ml/2½fl oz filtered water, or as needed to assist in blending
1–2 capsules of probiotic powder (content only)

1 Soak the cashew nuts for at least 3 hours. Discard the soaking water and rinse the nuts well.
2 Blend the nuts, salt and sugar in a blender or food processor until a smooth paste, adding water but as little as possible, just so that the blender will keep going. You should be able to get this blend completely smooth but it might take you some time as you do need to stop quite often to scrape down from the edges. If you have a high-speed blender you will be able to do this in just a few minutes.
3 When it has reached the desired consistency, scoop the mixture into a glass or ceramic bowl. Mix in the probiotic powder, stirring in well.
4 Leave the bowl to ferment at room temperature for 12–24 hours. Preferably it should be slightly warmer than your room, for example, in an airing cupboard or on the floor if you have underfloor heating or on top of your dehydrator if it is on. Otherwise just find the warmest place in your kitchen. It will work anyway, but might just take a bit longer.
5 When it is ready it should smell slightly sour or bread-like, and if you stir with a spoon it should be fluffy with air bubbles.
6 The fermented batch of cashew nut cheese can now be used. If you are not using it straight away you can keep it covered in the fridge. It will keep well for a few weeks in the fridge. It also freezes very well.

Matured Cashew Nut Cheese

You can age your nut cheese, just like normal cheese, for a more intense flavour. This is a very simple recipe but it is delicious. The nutritional yeast will give the nut cheese a typical cheesy flavour. Onion powder works beautifully as well, and has a sweet taste; the result is not the same if you use fresh onion. Pink salt, fresh rosemary and bay leaves make attractive decorations.

batch of fermented cashew nut cheese (see page 198)
7.5–15g/½–1 tbsp nutritional yeast powder
7.5g/½ tbsp onion powder
5g/1 tsp fine salt

1 Blend all the ingredients in a food processor or mix thoroughly by hand.
2 Turn out onto a board and shape your cheese how you want, using for example, a ring or biscuit cutter. If the dough is very runny it might not be mouldable – what you can do then is to keep it in the fridge for a while until it turns a bit harder, or just flavour it and use it as a dip or soft cheese. It is runny because you added too much water in your natural cashew cheese recipe; next time use less water.
3 Put the shapes into pieces of parchment paper, wrap them up and tie a string around. Or if you have a dehydrator you can put the cheeses (without parchment paper) here for a few hours at 42°C/107°F. This will give your cheeses a rind that will keep it together. Then wrap them with parchment and string.
4 Put in your fridge and keep it there for at least a few days to harden and mature. It is important not to cover the cheeses up, for example in a box with a lid. As they are very moist still they need to evaporate and if they are covered completely at this point they will stay soggy and perhaps mould will even start to grow. If you keep them in a box, do not put a lid on. You could put a kitchen towel or similar over to protect them if needed.
5 Your cheese is ready to be eaten in a few days. The longer you leave the cheese, the harder it will get and the more intense the flavour; 2–3 weeks is a good amount of time to give a fairly hard cheese that is easy to cut. I have let my nut cheeses mature for longer sometimes. Just be careful not to dry them out.
6 These cheeses store well in the fridge but do not put them in a covered box as they will get too damp and mould might start to grow. You can freeze these cheeses well for several months.

Fermented Macadamia or Almond Nut Cheese

There are two more nuts that I use to make nut cheeses with. You can get a much harder consistency of cheese with these, if that is what you are after, as you can press the nut paste when it is ready to get more water out. Pressing works better with almonds and macadamia nuts than cashews, though those will work if you take it slowly.

With almonds, you will have to soak them for the full soaking time and then let them sit in boiling water for 1–2 minutes. After that it is easy to take the skin off the nuts, although time-consuming. You can use blanched almonds instead of course. Blanched almonds have previously been heated whereas almonds with skins are often raw. Both versions ferment well.

Macadamia nuts make the most delicious cheese. They are easy to use as they don't have any skin to peel off, unlike almonds. However they are quite expensive and it is not so easy to find raw macadamia nuts, as they are often roasted.

250g/9oz macadamia or almond nuts
5ml/1 tsp agave syrup (optional)
pinch of sea salt
100ml/3½fl oz filtered water, or as needed to assist in blending
2 capsules of probiotic powder (content only)

1 Soak the nuts for 10–12 hours. Discard the soaking water and rinse the nuts well.
2 If you are using almonds with skins, then you now have to soak them further in boiling water for 1–2 minutes. Discard the boiling water and rinse the almonds with cold water to stop them from going soft. Then you can simply squeeze the almonds out of their skins between your fingers.
3 Put the nuts, agave if using, salt and water in a blender or food processor and process until a smooth consistency – you just need to add as much water as necessary to for the blades to go round. It doesn't matter if you add a little too much water however as we can get excess water out at a later stage. This processing might take a little while depending on what blender or food processor you have at home. I have a top-of-the-range food processor and it takes me only a few minutes. It is fine to use a normal food processor but be aware it can take as long as 5–10 minutes, so be patient, stopping your blender often to scrape down the sides.
4 When the desired consistency is reached, scoop the mixture into a glass or ceramic bowl and mix in the probiotic powder. Stir well to make sure it is fully dissolved in the mixture, then cover with a lid, cling film or a slightly damp cotton cloth.
5 Put the bowl in a warm place for 12–24 hours. This could be in an airing cupboard, on the floor if you have underfloor heating, or on top of your dehydrator if you have got one, or turn the light on in the oven and put it there, closing the door.
6 When it is ready it should have risen a little, smell slightly sour and if you stir with a wooden spoon it should be fluffy with air bubbles. Usually it takes 12 hours to ferment, but you might need to leave it for up to another 12 hours. Almonds and macadamia may take longer than cashews.
7 When ready, store it in the fridge. You can flavour it (see the following recipes), eat it straight away, or shape it into cheese shapes, wrap in parchment paper and store in the fridge for several days to mature.

8 If you want your almond or macadamia cheese to be harder in consistency you can do this by getting rid of excess water. This can be done before or after you flavour the cheese. Put the nut cheese in a cheese cloth or nut milk bag. Wring the cloth or bag so that the nut cheese sits tightly inside the cloth. If you squeeze it slightly you can see the water coming out. You don't want the water to come out too quickly as this will also bring out the cheese itself. The best way is to put the filled cloth or bag over a plastic colander placed over a bowl, put a plate over the cheese and then put something heavy on top of the plate to push the cheese down. Let it sit like this for 4–6 hours, allowing the weight to press the water through into the bowl underneath. The liquid should be clear, or you are pressing too hard. (This liquid, by the way, is nut whey and just like dairy whey it can be used as a starter for your next nut cheese instead of probiotic powder.) When ready take the cheese out of the cloth or bag and store it in the fridge, to be flavoured, eaten or wrapped to mature further.

Or, if you have a dehydrator, you can use this to dry the cheese. Make your preferred shape or shapes out of the nut cheese and put on to a dehydrator sheet. Dehydrate the cheese for about 4–6 hours at 42°C/107°F. This creates a rind around the cheese, making it harder and more handleable.

Paprika and Sun-dried Tomato Nut Cheese

This is a yummy nut cheese and you can make it using a batch of cashew cheese as well as with almond or macadamia cheese. The flavourings can be varied, I like to include a little harissa for heat. It is nice to decorate this cheese by dipping it in powdered paprika or mixed dried herbs.

batch of fermented macadamia or almond nut cheese (see page 202)
4–5 sun-dried tomatoes, chopped finely
15g/1 tbsp nutritional yeast powder
10g/2 tsp smoked paprika
5g/1 tsp sweet paprika, plus extra for dusting if liked
5g/1 tsp salt, or to taste
5g/1 tsp harissa paste
2.5g/½ tsp dried mixed Italian herbs, plus extra for dusting if liked

1 Make your batch of almond or macadamia cheese as described in the previous recipe, including the pressing stage in step 8 to get all the excess water out.
2 Put the nut cheese and all the listed ingredients into a food processor and pulse until blended together well. The cheese will have a slight pink tint to it now.
3 That's it! The cheese is now ready to mould into whatever shapes you want – little balls, rolls or rounds. You can decorate further, for example dipping the cheese into paprika powder or dried herbs.
4 If you like you can mature this cheese for a few days further in the fridge to deepen the flavour and make it even harder.

STAINLESS
STEEL

Garlic and Herb Nut Cheese Roll

This can be made with any of the three fermented nut cheeses. If you make it out of cashews, try to use as little water as possible when you blend the nuts. Again, the harder cheese you want, the longer you can mature it. This is another delicious nut cheese; if you put it on a platter with other cheeses your guests are unlikely to be able to tell that it is made from fermented nuts.

batch of fermented nut cheese (cashew, macadamia and almond, see page 198 or 202)
30g/2 tbsp nutritional yeast powder
15g/1 tbsp mixed dried herbs (thyme, rosemary and oregano for example), plus extra for decoration if liked
5g/1 tsp garlic powder
5g/1 tsp salt, or to taste

1 Mix all the ingredients together in a food processor, or mix thoroughly by hand.
2 Turn onto a board and mould the nut cheese into the size and shape you prefer. You can make one large or several small rolls, or other shapes using a ring mould, biscuit cutter or similar. You can sprinkle some dried herbs on top for decoration.
3 If you have a dehydrator you can dehydrate the cheese on 42°C/107°F for 4–6 hours to create a harder rind or crust on the cheese. Once dried, you can wrap in parchment paper and tie with string. If you don't have a dehydrator, wrap up in parchment paper and tie with string, and put into the fridge for a few days to harden and mature.
4 After a few days your cheese is ready to be eaten, but the longer you leave the cheese in the fridge the harder it will get and the more intense the flavour. You can leave it for several weeks if you want before eating it. Untouched, the cheese will last for 1–2 months. You can also freeze the cheese – nut cheeses freeze really well.

Bruna's Almond Cheese

My lovely Brazilian friend and colleague Bruna Oliveira has shared one of her amazing nut cheese recipes here. I met Bruna when we studied nutrition and naturopathy together, and we have since had many food adventures such as pop-up restaurants and cafés, catering, working at retreats and teaching courses.

- batch of fermented nut cheese, using almonds, pressed to remove extra water (see page 202, including step 8)
- 2.5g/½ tsp nutritional yeast powder
- 7.5g/1½ tsp miso paste
- 5g/1 tsp garlic powder
- 5ml/1 tsp lemon juice
- 7.5g/1½ tsp onion powder
- 5g/1 tsp salt
- 5g/1 tsp ground turmeric
- 2.5g/½ tsp powdered coconut sugar
- 2.5g/½ tsp mustard powder (optional)

1 Add the cheese to the rest of the ingredients in a bowl and mix everything together well.
2 Turn onto a board and shape the nut cheese, using a ring mould, biscuit cutter or similar. Decorate if you like, perhaps with sprigs of thyme.
3 If you have a dehydrator you can dehydrate the cheese on 42°C/107°F for 12 hours to create a harder rind or crust on the cheese. Once dried, wrap in parchment paper and tie with string, and transfer to the fridge. If you don't have a dehydrator, wrap up in parchment paper and tie with string, and put into the fridge for a few days to harden and mature.
4 After a few days your cheese is ready to be eaten, but the longer you leave the cheese in the fridge the harder it will get and the more intense the flavour. It will keep for at least a month if unopened.

Cashew Yogurt

This is a bit like making a cashew nut cheese, but adding more water. It can be enjoyed just like your normal yogurt, perhaps with granola and berries. It can also be made into a dressing or a sauce; just add spices of your choice.

250g/9oz cashews, soaked for at least 2 hours and rinsed
10ml/2 tsp powdered coconut sugar
pinch of salt
1 probiotic capsule (content only)
150–250ml/5¼–8¾fl oz filtered water, as needed

1 Add all the ingredients apart from the probiotic to a high-speed blender and blend until it reaches the desired creamy consistency. Add just half the water first, then add more as needed to blend to the consistency you like.
2 Add the probiotic powder and blend in, or stir it in by hand.
3 Pour the nut cream into a glass or ceramic bowl and cover with cling film or plastic wrap, or a wet cotton cloth. Make sure there is a gap of a few cm/inches so that the cream can expand.
4 Let the creamy yogurt ferment, at room temperature or slightly warmer, for 24 hours. Check after 24 hours and if you would like it more sour-tasting, ferment for another 12–24 hours.
5 When done, enjoy it straight away or store in sealed jars in the fridge. It will keep for about a week after opening.

Coconut Yogurt

Deliciously creamy and decadent. Add to granola, apple and berries and eat for breakfast, perhaps with a drizzle of coconut syrup, or treat as a cream and pour over a homemade crumble or cake. Make sure the can of coconut is a brand that does not include any ingredients other than coconut, water and salt, and no preservatives. Choose full-fat or whole coconut milk; diet or low-fat coconut milk will not work well.

400ml/14fl oz can of coconut milk, chilled for 24 hours
5g/1 tsp powdered coconut sugar
1 probiotic capsule (content only)

1 The can of coconut is refrigerated so that the liquid separates from the solids. Open the can and pour only the liquid into a glass – do not throw it away. Pour or scoop the semi-solid coconut cream into a separate glass or ceramic bowl.
2 Add the coconut liquid to the cream, stirring in bit by bit until you have the consistency you prefer. Mix together well.
3 Add the sugar and the probiotic capsule content into the yogurt, and mix well. Cover with cling film or plastic wrap, or a wet cotton cloth.
4 Let the creamy yogurt ferment, at room temperature or slightly warmer, for 24 hours. Check after 24 hours and if you would like it more sour-tasting, ferment for another 12–24 hours.
5 When ready, eat straight away or store in the fridge. It will keep for at least a week.

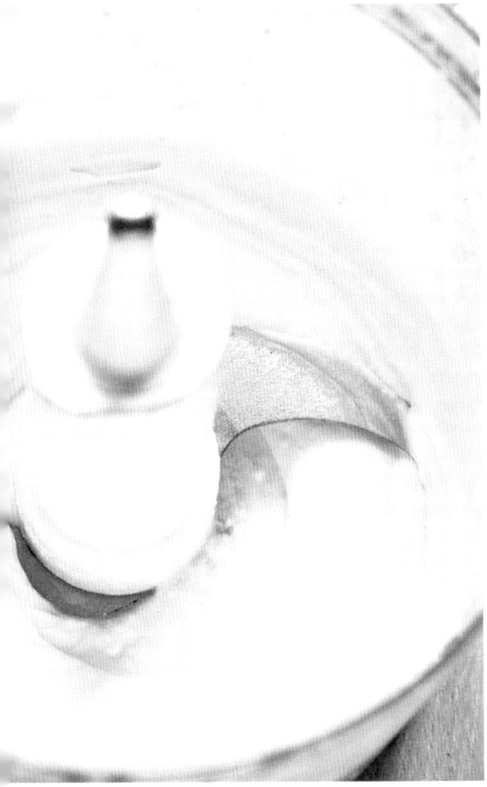

Coconut Milk Kefir

If you have dairy kefir or milk kefir grains, you can also make kefir out of non-dairy milk. You do still need to feed your milk kefir grains with normal cow's milk now and then, but with very active kefir grains it is possible to then use them to make non-dairy kefir as well. Make sure the can of coconut is a brand that does not include any ingredients other than coconut, water and salt, and no preservatives. Choose full-fat or whole coconut milk; diet or low-fat will not work well. You can also make coconut water kefir, see page 161.

400ml/14fl oz can of coconut milk
30–45g/2–3 tbsp active dairy kefir grains

1 Pour the canned coconut milk into a blender to mix together the liquid and solids to a creamy consistency.
2 Pour the blended coconut milk into a fermentation jar. The jar or bottle should be at least 600ml or 1 pint, with a tight-fitting lid. Add the milk kefir grains. Put on the lid and turn it upside down a few times to mix again.
3 Let ferment for 2–3 days, turning the jar upside down a few times and also opening it up every day to let any gases out. It should smell pleasant and sour when fermented, and also taste a little sour like yogurt.
4 When ready, strain out the grains using a plastic sieve – it is important that the strainer is not made of metal. Keep the grains for the next batch and pour the fermented milk or kefir into glass jars.
5 Store the kefir in the fridge; it will keep for several weeks.
6 The grains need to go into your next batch of kefir, or if not being used for a while they will keep in the fridge stored in some dairy milk for several weeks. However, to keep the grains active it is not good to store them too long. See pages 180–3 for more details about kefir grains.

Raw Chocolate Cashew Cheesecake

This is an incredibly easy cheesecake to make and it's super-delicious with a lovely consistency. Vegan, gluten-free, sugar-free and dairy-free, but your friends will never guess.

250g/9oz coconut, fresh or raw desiccated
225g/8oz mixed nuts of your choice, chopped roughly
200g/7oz fresh dates
batch of fermented cashew nut cheese (see page 198)
100ml/3½fl oz agave syrup
100ml/3½fl oz coconut oil, melted
15ml/1 tbsp fresh lemon juice (optional)
2.5ml/½ tsp tamari (optional, to bring the flavour out)
80g/2¾oz raw cacao powder
a few fresh raspberries, to decorate (optional)

20–23-CM/8–9-INCH CAKE

1 Make the crust by first putting the coconut and nuts in a food processor and processing a little.
2 Chop, stone and add the fresh dates to the coconut, and process again to form a dough-like texture.
3 Line a cake dish with cling film or plastic wrap – or use a silicone dish. Press the dough into the dish to make the crust base for your cheesecake. Put into the fridge or freezer while you make the filling.
4 To make the filling, put the remaining ingredients except the cacao powder into a high-speed blender or food processor and blend until it is all mixed and smooth. Then, add the cacao powder and stir to blend in.
5 Pour the filling into the crust and smooth out with a spatula.
6 Place the cake in the freezer for 2–4 hours so the coconut oil sets.
7 Take out the cheesecake, and decorate with a few fresh raspberries if you like before serving. If not eaten straight away, store it in the fridge, where it will keep for a week at least.

Note: Your filling will have a coconut flavour to it as well as chocolate. If you do not want the coconut flavour you can use odour-free coconut, which has has been slightly more processed to get rid of the taste and smell of coconut.

CHAPTER NINE:

Fermented Baking

Many culinary traditions ferment their grains in one way or another. It is not the same as vegetable fermentation because it involves a completely different lactic acid bacteria called *Lactobacillus sanfranciscensis* which lives in symbiosis with a yeast called *Candida humilis*.

Grains are a great staple wholefood that we should include in our diet as long as they are not refined. White flour is processed so much that there are few nutrients left, which means the manufacturers have to add back artificially-made vitamins and minerals to be able to sell it as a food. Grains can also be hard to digest for many people, and can benefit greatly from a fermentation process.

Sprouting or fermenting your grains before eating them will make them more digestible, increase the protein content, increase other nutrients, and make these nutrients more bioavailable. For an example of this, grains contain phytic acid, which is a compound, also found in nuts and pulses, believed to inhibit the absorption of important minerals. By soaking, sprouting or fermenting grains, phytic acid will be mostly eliminated. Grains also contain enzyme inhibitors that will greatly be eliminated by fermentation. All in all, fermenting or sprouting your grains before eating them seems a good idea for health reasons.

To sprout a grain means to germinate it; grain is simply soaked in water and left until a little shoot grows from it. Before sprouting, the grain is a good wholefood, but after sprouting it becomes an incredible superfood. I like to make my own flour from sprouted grains and then make a fermented loaf of bread from it. This takes time, but you end up with a delicious bread that you know will be very nourishing. Instead of seeing it as a time-consuming way of making bread, see it as a way to relax and be creative. If you are in a positive mood when you make food it will transfer to the results!

Many people are sensitive to wheat, but you might find that this flour doesn't affect you in the same way; many of my clients discover they are fine with eating breads made from sprouted wheat flour, whereas they would instantly bloat from eating a shop-bought bread.

This chapter is quite short and features just a couple of fermented bread recipes, including of course sourdough, as examples of the many amazing bakes you can make with sprouted and fermented grain. I give the method for making sprouted flour, and a sourdough starter (shown opposite). The sprouted flour can be used like any other flour, in breads, cakes, sauces and pancakes. Wheat berries are used here but you can also sprout oat berries, spelt berries, rye berries, kamut berries, and einkorn berries.

Sprouted Wheatflour

Sprouting grains turns them into a nutritional powerhouse, and grinding them into flour take these benefits into your baking. I dry the sprouted grains in my dehydrator, which does give the best results. If you live in a warm country with low humidity you can dry them in the sun! If you use a conventional oven I suggest using a low heat like 100°C/212°F and to make sure the oven door is open so that moisture can get out. It will take a couple of hours to dry completely. This sprouted flour can also be made with other grains, like spelt, oat, kamut, einkorn and rye.

2kg/4½lb whole organic wheat berries

1 Place the grains in a large glass jar or bowl and add filtered water to cover the grains and a bit more, so that the grains can swell and still be completely covered.
2 Leave at room temperature for 36–48 hours. During this time, the grains should have grown tiny little sprouts and the water will be slightly bubbly. As soon as this happens, they are done.
3 Rinse the sprouts well and discard the water.
4 Place the grains in a dehydrator at 42°C/107°F for 12 hours until completely dry. Or if you do not have a dehydrator you could do it in the oven at 100°C/212°F for 2 hours with the oven door open. Make sure the grains are completely dry.
5 Grind the dried sprouted wheat berries in a mill or good blender or food processor. The sprouted flour is now ready, to be used as you would any plain or all-purpose flour. Store in an airtight container.

Sourdough Starter

I was brought up on homemade sourdough breads. In Sweden, we are very keen on sourdough breads and even commercial breads found in the big supermarkets are often made from sourdough starter rather than yeast. I have avoided wheat and gluten for almost 20 years; however, I have discovered that I now can eat gluten without my digestive system going crazy so nowadays I love to eat sourdough bread.

To be able to make sourdough bread you need to have a sourdough starter. You can buy these from some speciality shops but it is really easy to make your own. A good sourdough starter can keep going for many years. Some sourdough bakeries have starters going back decades. If you are lucky enough to know a sourdough baker you could ask them if they can give you some of their starter; professional bakers might not share their starters but most home bakers will be delighted to impress you with theirs.

If you bake often, you can have your sourdough starter out at room temperature, feeding it daily or at least every other day. To feed it means to add more flour and water.

If you are not baking often you can put the starter in the fridge, in a sealed container. When you are ready to bake again you will need to wake it up a day or two beforehand. To do this, take it out of the fridge, feed it and put it somewhere warm – perhaps on the floor if you have underfloor heating, or turn the light on in the oven and put it in the oven with the door closed. The starter will be ready again when it rises a little and gets a bit bubbly.

I recommend rye flour, and adding a little grated apple for sweetness and to help fermentation, although you can leave this out if you prefer.

DAY 1:

100g/3½oz organic rye or wheat flour

75–100ml/2½–3½fl oz filtered water

50g/1¾oz grated organic apple (optional – if including, use 75ml/3½fl oz water only)

DAYS 3 AND 4:

100g/3½oz organic rye or wheat flour

50ml/1¾fl oz filtered water

Day 1 In a clean glass jar with a lid, add the flour and water, and grated apple if using, and stir well. Put the lid on and leave at room temperature.

Day 2 Stir the contents of the jar with a wooden utensil. Replace the lid and store again at room temperature.

Day 3 Stir in the additional flour and water. Leave at room temperature for another day.

Day 4 The dough has probably risen a little and you should see the bubbles and notice a sour smell, slightly vinegary but not unpleasant. This is a sign it is almost done. Add the flour and water again and stir. Leave at room temperature for another day.

Day 5 If not before, you should definitely see bubbles by now. The sourdough starter is now ready to use.

Sprouted Buckwheat Loaf

Buckwheat is an amazing gluten-free grain. The name can slightly mislead as it is not related to wheat at all. And to confuse you even more it is not even a grain but instead a fruit-seed. However, it is used as a grain. Buckwheat is high in protein, making it a good alternative to other grains. It is also an excellent source of magnesium, fibre, copper, phosphorus and quercetin (which is a great antioxidant).

400g/14oz raw buckwheat

350ml/12¼fl oz filtered water, kefir water, kombucha or a mixture

100ml/3½fl oz milk kefir (optional; if you do use it, omit the same amount of liquid)

15–30g/1–2 tbsp mixed dried or fresh herbs

5g/1 tsp salt

100g/3½oz mixed seeds (sunflower, pumpkin, shelled hemp)

1 Soak the buckwheat for 7 hours, changing the water at least once during this time. When soaked, discard the water and rinse the buckwheat thoroughly. The water coming out will be slightly pink and slimy; you need to rinse until this disappears.
2 Sprout the buckwheat in filtered water for 24 hours, rinsing them as often as you can. If you can see little tails grow out before 24 hours are up, they are ready, so do check them regularly. Do a last rinse very thoroughly.
3 Put the sprouted buckwheat in a blender or food processor. Add the measured water and/or kefirs, the herbs and the salt, and process to a dough-like consistency.
4 Transfer the dough to a glass bowl, cover and leave it at room temperature or slightly warmer for 7 hours. When ready, it should have risen a little and when you stir it should be bubbly and smell a little bit sour. If there are no bubbles formed, let it ferment for another couple of hours.
5 When ready, stir in the seeds, keeping a handful back.
6 Line a loaf tin or bread pan with parchment paper, scatter in the remaining seeds over the base, and pour the fermented dough into the pan. You can let the dough stand and ferment for another couple of hours or you can put it straight in the oven. I normally let it ferment again.
7 Set the oven for 170°C/338°F. If you don't let the bread ferment a second time you can leave it in the oven while it warms up.
8 Bake the bread for 60 minutes at the stated temperature.
9 When ready, take the bread out of the oven and let it cool for at least half an hour before you cut it up. The bread is best eaten while it is fresh. Put in the fridge if not eaten straight away, where it will keep for a week.

Lotta's Spelt Sourdough Baguettes

My friend Lotta is a Swedish nurse and mum of five children, living in New York. We met at university in Sweden many years ago. We share a keen interest in health and food and have followed a similar path in life even though we don't see each other much. She has been making sourdough bread daily for her large family for the last 20-plus years and if anyone knows about sourdough home baking, it is her. When I asked her to share her favourite recipe with me for this book I was absolutely delighted when she said yes.

For best results use a food mixer or dough mixer. You might have it already as part of your food processor. Or if you have a kitchen aid or a Thermomix this is ideal. Alternatively, you can knead by hand, folding the dough into the middle of itself, pushing it down, and repeating.

250g/9oz rolled oats
600ml/1 pint cold filtered water
150ml/5¼fl oz sourdough starter (see page 224)
15ml/1 tbsp raw honey
1–1.5kg/2¼–3¼lb white spelt flour (you can swap some for wholemeal spelt if you prefer)
10g/2 tsp salt

1 Mix the oats, water, sourdough starter and honey in a large bowl. Do not add the salt.

2 Add the flour little by little, mixing it well with your hands. The dough should be thick in consistency but still a tiny bit sticky when you are done with it. It must not be dry.

3a If you have a dough mixer, add the dough to the mixer bowl with a dough hook and process on a low speed for about 7 minutes. Add the salt and possibly some more flour to the dough and work it in for another 5 minutes on a higher speed.

3b If you haven't got a dough mixer, add some more flour as you don't want it too sticky on your hands. Now add the salt. Knead the dough by hand by folding the dough into itself and then pushing it down. Repeat just like that for 10–15 minutes, folding it to the middle, pushing it down. By kneading the dough, you will develop the gluten that makes the bread airy, light, fluffy and chewy. Without it, your bread will be flat and dense.

4 Put the dough in a large oiled plastic container with a lid and put in the fridge to proof overnight.

5 In the morning, heat the oven to 250°C/482°F. Tip the dough out onto a floured surface and divide into three. Very lightly twist and make three long baguettes. Place them carefully on an oven plate covered with parchment paper.

6 Bake them in the oven for 15 minutes. Open the oven once or twice during this time to spray the baguettes with some water.

7 After 15 minutes, lower the temperature to 150°C/302°F and bake for another 15 minutes. Open the oven once or twice during this time to spray the baguettes again. When the breads are ready they should sound hollow when knocking on the bottom of the bread.

8 Take the breads out and let them cool on a wire rack underneath a cotton cloth. The bread is now ready to eat.

Troubleshooting Q&A

THE PROBLEM	REASON WHY IT HAS HAPPENED	POTENTIAL SOLUTION
My sauerkraut, pickles or kimchi are all soft and mushy	This could be a number of things. Most commonly it is due to too little salt; salt will keep the vegetables crunchy, so if you don't use salt or use too little they can become soft. Too high a temperature during fermentation is another possible cause; the ideal temperature is 18–20°C/64.5–68°F. Or, if less commonly the reason, perhaps the vegetables you are using are too old or non-organic.	It is perfectly safe to eat soft sauerkraut, but if you don't like it you could use it in cooking.
My ferment is slimy	This is due to either fermenting in too high a temperature or using too little or no salt.	This is most probably the beginning of a rot. I would throw this kraut in the compost bin.
There is a white foam or scum on top of my ferment	This can happen when the vegetables are exposed to air. Perhaps you did not have a good enough jar with a tight-fitting lid to ferment in. Or you opened the lid a bit too often and for a bit too long.	Just skim the foam off the surface and scoop the top layer of the ferment out and throw away. The rest should be fine.
There is a white cloudy layer floating on top of my ferment	This is top yeast or Kahm yeast, and is often mistaken for mould. Kahm yeast is white in colour and appears to float on liquid in a thin layer. Mould is different, coming in a variety of colours (often green) and is not floating on liquid.	Top yeast is not dangerous, but it means that your ferment will not keep for long, so eat it straight away or use it in cooking. If this is seen on your newly fermented sauerkraut, just scrape the top off and the rest should be fine.
There is mould on or in my fermented vegetables	Check it is definitely not Kahm yeast, explained above; mould is often multicoloured with lots of green or blue, it can be furry, and it smells like mould. Mould can happen when the fermenting environment has not been anaerobic, and unwanted bacteria has been able to interfere. Your fermentation jar might not have had a tight-enough lid so oxygen has been let in. It could also be because of bad hygiene, or possibly you are fermenting in a room that has a mould or mildew problem.	It is likely that the mould is only on the surface and whatever has been fermenting under the water surface is fine and mould-free. Some fermentation professionals argue that It is safe to scrape the top mould away and eat what is underneath as long as it has been under the water. I would personally throw the ferment away, and try and work out why it was mouldy to do the necessary adjustments next time.
My ferment is too salty	This often happens if you don't measure your salt. In the beginning do follow the recommended amount of 1.5–2% salt for dry-salt ferments and 3–5% for brine ferments.	You could try and wash your kraut in water to get some of the salt off. Or mix it with another kraut that is less salty. You could also perhaps use it in cooking. Make a coleslaw out of it; adding lots of fresh cabbage to make it less salty might work well.

My fermentation jar is leaking from the top	Basically, you have put too much vegetable in the jar. You need to leave a larger gap next time so that the gases can come out and vegetables can expand a little. You might also have forgotten to burp your jar.	You might want to take some of the kraut out. Open the lid to let gases out and burp more regularly. Put your jar on a plate for the rest of the fermentation to catch liquid coming out.
My fermented vegetables smell rotten	This depends if the smell is just when you open the lid, or continual. If only when you open the lid it is probably just the smell of sulphur from the cabbage, which is normal. Fermented foods have a specific kind of smell that you need to get used to. If it smells the whole time it probably is rotten. Sometimes non-organic vegetables rot rather than ferment. Also, it can happen if no or very little salt has been used.	If it is properly rotten and not just the normal sulphur smell of sauerkraut, there is only one thing to do with it. Throw it in the compost bin.
My kraut is changing colour	It is normal for the kraut to change colour slightly. White cabbage mixed with red for example will take the same colour as the red cabbage during the fermentation process. If you add fresh turmeric to white cabbage the cabbage will eventually all turn the same yellow colour. However, sometimes white cabbage turns pink or red cabbage turns brown. This might be because you have used too little salt, or in some cases too much salt, or if you used a cooking or table salt with iodine added. It might be yeast causing the colour as well.	Unless it has changed colour for the obvious natural reasons as explained, you might want to actually throw this kraut away just to be safe.
My ferment exploded	This is very rare! But you must be careful to check on your ferment regularly and to burp it to release the built-up gases. If you are using a jar with a tight lid, like a screw-on lid, there is more risk of pressure building up.	Remember to burp your jar, or if you aren't sure you will remember to open it up regularly to let the gases out, do use a proper fermentation jar with a suitable lid or a bespoke fermentation crockpot.

Troubleshooting Fermented Drinks

My fermented drink tastes 'off' or mouldy	This is not common, but it means that there is probably mould in your drink or it has gone off one way or another. Perhaps you kept your scoby/grains in the fridge for a long time and just taken it out to start making drinks again. Or you have fermented it for too long or at too high a temperature. Perhaps you used fresh fruit or berries and left them in for a long time.	For the drink – throw it out! If you are using fruit or berries then strain the drink of bits of fruit as soon as you can. You might still need a new scoby or new grains. Also, always be careful with hygiene.

My fermented drinks have no bubbles or fizz	Fizz happens over time and it is the second fermentation that normally fizzes a drink up. Water kefir gets more fizzy than kombucha. With kombucha, not enough fizz can happen when your scoby is new or has been kept in the fridge without using for a while. Temperature matters as well. Or perhaps it is the type of scoby or starter you use.	Don't worry, to make the drink more fizzy, you can do a second fermentation and let it sit in a 100% air-sealed bottle at room temperature for 24 hours. The last bit of sugar in your drink will then turn into fizz. Add some fresh fruit juice or fruit purée, or add a little bit of sugar, and let it sit at room temperature in a sealed bottle for 24 hours without the kombucha scoby or kefir grains. If it is still not fizzy enough after 24 hours you can leave it for another 24 hours. Another note, if making kombucha you should not filter out any small bits of the scoby.
My water kefir grains look like they have melted	This can happen because you have fermented for too long or at too hot a temperature. In the summer the room may be warmer and kefir can ferment very quickly, in less than 24 hours sometimes.	The grains are probably on the way to die and you need to look for some new ones. When they die they start to disintegrate.
My water kefir grains are not growing	If you just got your water grains they can take a little while to grow. You need to really get into kefir making for it to work properly. Get into a flow of constantly making a new batch and not leaving the grains unfed. Leave your kefir to ferment no longer than 48 hours. If it is still very sweet you need to take the grains out and let it ferment further without the grains. Only when you get into a good rhythm of making kefir water will they start to multiply. Also, make sure you have the right ratios of sugar, water and grains.	Go back and look at the tips on how to look after your grains in the water kefir section in this book, and feed them with minerals, ginger, fruit and unrefined sweeteners. However, if they are producing a good water kefir still I would not worry about it. Just keep doing what you are doing. Eventually they will start to multiply.
My kefir water is not fermenting and is still sweet after several days	Your water kefir grains are probably dead or dying. Perhaps you forgot them in your last batch and they fermented for several days. Or perhaps you have had the grains in the fridge for a longer period. Or it's the warm season so temperatures are high. Refer to the kefir section on page 150, and feed them with what they like.	You probably need to get some new grains. You could try and reactivate them by changing the water every 24 hours even though it is still sweet. Also see the tips on how to look after your grains in the water by, for example, feeding them ginger, minerals and fresh turmeric.
My kefir water has got a slimy texture to it	This could be a too-high temperature whilst fermenting, or your grains are on the way out. You might read somewhere it is due to too much mineral in the liquid. This is not the case in my experience, but worth bearing in mind.	Pour it out and start again, to try and revive the grains. You might have to get new grains however.

My kombucha scoby is looking very strange, with an assortment of colours	A kombucha scoby is an odd thing. It can take on a brownish colour with darker bits here and there, or it can be very light. It depends on where you got it from. Don't be scared of your kombucha scoby. You need to be nice to it, and don't let it sit in your fridge for too long without feeding it.	It is probably fine the way it is so continue to use it. If you are really worried that it is not in a good way, throw it in the compost and get yourself a new one.
My kombucha scoby has a white thin layer on top of it	This is probably a new baby scoby. You can leave it where it is or peel it off carefully and use it as a scoby in its own right.	All is well and you can continue to use your scoby.

Troubleshooting Nut Dairy

My cheese has been fermenting for 24 hours and is still not bubbly or smelling sour	Did you forget to add a starter? Or perhaps the starter you were using was not good enough. Maybe it was old, or maybe you didn't add enough. All starters are different and you might need more even though you followed the recipe. You might also have fermented it in too cold a temperature.	Let it ferment for another 12–24 hours to see if it works. Otherwise try again using another starter or add more of the starter to the ferment. I find when I use a good probiotic capsule it normally works very well. I have had occasional problems with other starters, but never with the probiotic powder.
I have pressed my almond cheese overnight but it is still soft	You are either not pressing it hard enough or there was just too much water to start with.	Press it for a bit longer and a little harder. Next time try to use less water in your recipe. If your blender does not mix easily unless you use a lot of water you might want to think about investing in a better heavy-duty one. You can also invest in a cheese press.
There is crust on the surface of my fermented cheese	This can happen when it dries because of the air and oxygen.	If you don't want this to happen use cling film or plastic wrap to cover the cheese with when it is fermenting. Make some holes in the plastic so that the air can come out. Another option is to scrape the crust off the surface, but there is no danger in keeping it either.
I can't get my cheese very smooth, even though I have been processing it for a long time	Probably your blender or food processor isn't very good.	Add more water to your blender; you also need to regularly stop it to scrape down the sides, blend, and then stop and scrape again. If that doesn't work you might want to invest in a better heavy-duty blender.

Nutritional Notes

p60, Aunt Birgitta's sauerkraut (1.5ltr) Energy 354kcal/1499kJ; Protein 18.2g; Carbohydrate 73.1g, of which sugars 69.1g; Fat 7.7g, of which saturates 0.2g; Cholesterol 0mg; Calcium 899mg; Fibre 40.7g; Sodium 5989mg.

p62, Swedish summer kraut (1.5ltr) Energy 355kcal/1496kJ; Protein 17g; Carbohydrate 68.7g, of which sugars 62.8g; Fat 6.6g, of which saturates 0.5g; Cholesterol 0mg; Calcium 829mg; Fibre 45.6g; Sodium 6058mg.

p64, Fresh turmeric kraut (1.5ltr) Energy 315kcal/1328kJ; Protein 14.6g; Carbohydrate 60.7g, of which sugars 55.2g; Fat 5.7g, of which saturates 0.4g; Cholesterol 0mg; Calcium 773mg; Fibre 42.9g; Sodium 6065mg.

p66, Carrot, ginger and cumin kraut (1ltr) Energy 350kcal/1460kJ; Protein 11.3g; Carbohydrate 79g, of which sugars 74g; Fat 8.5g, of which saturates 1.3g; Cholesterol 0mg; Calcium 542mg; Fibre 32g; Sodium 6190mg.

p68, Mixed root kraut (1ltr) Energy 352kcal/1478kJ; Protein 10.8g; Carbohydrate 69.2g, of which sugars 49.5g; Fat 5.2g, of which saturates 0.8g; Cholesterol 0mg; Calcium 399mg; Fibre 42g; Sodium 6248mg.

p70, Sweet beetroot kraut (1ltr) Energy 180kcal/770kJ; Protein 8.5g; Carbohydrate 38g, of which sugars 35g; Fat 0.5g, of which saturates 0g; Cholesterol 0mg; Calcium 101mg; Fibre 12.7g; Sodium 4260mg.

p72, Beetroot and cabbage kraut (1.5ltr) Energy 285kcal/1215kJ; Protein 14g; Carbohydrate 56.5g, of which sugars 51.5g; Fat 2g, of which saturates 0g; Cholesterol 0mg; Calcium 402mg; Fibre 29.3g; Sodium 6265mg.

p74, Fennel, chilli and celery kraut (1.5ltr) Energy 125kcal/524kJ; Protein 11.4g; Carbohydrate 19.1g, of which sugars 18.3g; Fat 4.3g, of which saturates 0.1g; Cholesterol 0mg; Calcium 486mg; Fibre 28.5g; Sodium 6143mg.

p76, Curried cauliflower kraut (1.5ltr) Energy 372kcal/1559kJ; Protein 33.4g; Carbohydrate 37.9g, of which sugars 26.6g; Fat 10.5g, of which saturates 1.6g; Cholesterol 0mg; Calcium 450mg; Fibre 33.5g; Sodium 6096mg.

p82, Low-salt sauerkraut (1.5ltr) Energy 304kcal/1287kJ; Protein 12.4g; Carbohydrate 58.1g, of which sugars 55.5g; Fat 4g, of which saturates 0.3g; Cholesterol 0mg; Calcium 564mg; Fibre 30.3g; Sodium 2193mg.

p84, Cauliflower, carrot and onion pickles (1.5ltr) Energy 348kcal/1452kJ; Protein 19.2g; Carbohydrate 59.4g, of which sugars 50.8g; Fat 5.2g, of which saturates 1.2g; Cholesterol 0mg; Calcium 235mg; Fibre 26.1g; Sodium 4072mg.

p86, Fermented Swedish cucumber (2ltr) Energy 126kcal/510kJ; Protein 7.5g; Carbohydrate 20.9g, of which sugars 19.6g; Fat 1.2g, of which saturates 0.1g; Cholesterol 0mg; Calcium 200mg; Fibre 10.4g; Sodium 3979mg.

p88, Green beans with dill (1–1.5ltr) Energy 130kcal/536kJ; Protein 10.3g; Carbohydrate 17.6g, of which sugars 11.7g; Fat 2.6g, of which saturates 0.5g; Cholesterol 0mg; Calcium 182mg; Fibre 15.2g; Sodium 1965mg.

p90, Sour tomatoes with rosemary and thyme (1.5-ltr) Energy 223kcal/952kJ; Protein 8.3g; Carbohydrate 42.9g, of which sugars 40.8g; Fat 3.4g, of which saturates 1.1g; Cholesterol 0mg; Calcium 108mg; Fibre 17.1g; Sodium 4041mg.

p92, Mixed pickles (1.5ltr) Energy 280kcal/1175kJ; Protein 8.5g; Carbohydrate 58g, of which sugars 53.5g; Fat 3g, of which saturates 0.5g; Cholesterol 0mg; Calcium 426mg; Fibre 32.7g; Sodium 6060mg.

p94, Fermented wild garlic (300ml) Energy 62kcal/258kJ; Protein 7g; Carbohydrate 4g, of which sugars 3.8g; Fat 2g, of which saturates 0.2g; Cholesterol 0mg; Calcium 426mg; Fibre 7g; Sodium 2315mg.

p96, Fermented rhubarb (1–1.5ltr) Energy 42kcal/191kJ; Protein 4.8g; Carbohydrate 5.4g, of which sugars 4.5g; Fat 0.6g, of which saturates 0g; Cholesterol 0mg; Calcium 468mg; Fibre 9.3g; Sodium 1982mg.

p98, Pickled chillies (1ltr) Energy 166kcal/695kJ; Protein 10.2g; Carbohydrate 28.9g, of which sugars 26.6g; Fat 1.7g, of which saturates 0g; Cholesterol 0mg; Calcium 106mg; Fibre 1.9g; Sodium 3010mg.

p106, Kimchi paste (300ml) Energy 479kcal/2010kJ; Protein 18.4g; Carbohydrate 88.4g, of which sugars 53.7g; Fat 9.6g, of which saturates 1.4g; Cholesterol 0mg; Calcium 164mg; Fibre 1.6g; Sodium 4727mg.

p108, Asa's kimchi (1.5ltr) Energy 316kcal/1312kJ; Protein 16.5g; Carbohydrate 53.6g, of which sugars 47.1g; Fat 4.5g, of which saturates 0.5g; Cholesterol 0mg; Calcium 707mg; Fibre 24.1g; Sodium 6821mg.

p110, Cucumber kimchi (1.5ltr) Energy 100kcal/416kJ; Protein 4.1g; Carbohydrate 18.7g, of which sugars 14.6g; Fat 1.5g, of which saturates 0.2g; Cholesterol 0mg; Calcium 81mg; Fibre 4.6g; Sodium 2476mg.

p112, Curried kimchi (1.5ltr) Energy 521kcal/2181kJ; Protein 32.8g; Carbohydrate 71g, of which sugars 42.5g; Fat 12.7g, of which saturates 1.2g; Cholesterol 0mg; Calcium 650mg; Fibre 28.4g; Sodium 3108mg.

p114, Mooli kimchi (1.5ltr) Energy 307kcal/1298kJ; Protein 14.8g; Carbohydrate 65.7g, of which sugars 60.2g; Fat 6.9g, of which saturates 0.2g; Cholesterol 0mg; Calcium 422mg; Fibre 1.5g; Sodium 3567mg.

p115, Korean kimchi with fish sauce (1ltr) Energy 225kcal/932kJ; Protein 14.4g; Carbohydrate 37.2g, of which sugars 32.2g; Fat 4.4g, of which saturates 0.3g; Cholesterol 0mg; Calcium 558mg; Fibre 22.4g; Sodium 1299mg.

p122, Tomato and coriander salsa (1ltr) Energy 212kcal/900kJ; Protein 12.3g; Carbohydrate 39g, of which sugars 35.2g; Fat 6g, of which saturates 1g; Cholesterol 0mg; Calcium 318mg; Fibre 14.9g; Sodium 6014mg.

p124, Cultured spicy ketchup (600ml) Energy 465kcal/1959kJ; Protein 18g; Carbohydrate 90.8g, of which sugars 78.7g; Fat 5.3g, of which saturates 0.7g; Cholesterol 0mg; Calcium 183mg; Fibre 11.2g; Sodium 733mg.

p126, Spicy pear and pecan chutney (1ltr) Energy 1571kcal/6594kJ; Protein 18.5g; Carbohydrate 228.3g, of which sugars 226.8g; Fat 72.5g, of which saturates 5.9g; Cholesterol 0mg; Calcium 619mg; Fibre 36.9g; Sodium 2074mg.

p128, Spicy chilli salsa (1ltr) Energy 544kcal/2279kJ; Protein 16.3g; Carbohydrate 119.5g, of which sugars 44.9g; Fat 3.1g, of which saturates 0g; Cholesterol 0mg; Calcium 144mg; Fibre 0.3g; Sodium 2077mg.

p130, Fermented berry jam (300ml) Energy 371kcal/1559kJ; Protein 2.2g; Carbohydrate 94.8g, of which sugars 28.4g; Fat 1.2g, of which saturates 0.1g; Cholesterol 0mg; Calcium 38mg; Fibre 10g; Sodium 992mg.

p132, Preserved lemons (1ltr) Energy 152kcal/632kJ; Protein 8g; Carbohydrate 25.6g, of which sugars 25.6g; Fat 2.4g, of which saturates 0.8g; Cholesterol 0mg; Calcium 685mg; Fibre 0g; Sodium 19690mg.

p142, Simple kombucha (2.5ltr) Energy 1182kcal/5080kJ; Protein 2g; Carbohydrate 315g, of which sugars 315g; Fat 0g, of which saturates 0g; Cholesterol 0mg; Calcium 30mg; Fibre 0g; Sodium 15mg.

p144, Raspberry and apricot kombucha (1ltr) Energy 643kcal/2764kJ; Protein 5.7g; Carbohydrate 164.4g, of which sugars 164.4g; Fat 0.9g, of which saturates 0.2g; Cholesterol 0mg; Calcium 100mg; Fibre 10.9g; Sodium 20mg.

p146, Grapefuit, orange and thyme kombucha (1ltr) Energy 471kcal/2020kJ; Protein 1.8g; Carbohydrate 124g, of which sugars 124g; Fat 0.2g, of which saturates 0g; Cholesterol 0mg; Calcium 41mg; Fibre 0.1g; Sodium 25mg.

p148, Apple and elderflower kombucha (1ltr) Energy 480kcal/2067kJ; Protein 0.9g; Carbohydrate 127.5g, of which sugars 127.5g; Fat 0.2g, of which saturates 0g; Cholesterol 0mg; Calcium 27mg; Fibre 0g; Sodium 10mg.

p154, Simple lemon water kefir (1.5ltr) Energy 391kcal/1660kJ; Protein 11.6g; Carbohydrate 87.2g, of which sugars 87g; Fat 1g, of which saturates 0g; Cholesterol 0mg; Calcium 416mg; Fibre 0.1g; Sodium 4mg.

p156, Apple and beetroot juice kefir (1.5ltr) Energy 490kcal/2100kJ; Protein 12g; Carbohydrate 111.9g, of which sugars 111.6g; Fat 2g, of which saturates 0g; Cholesterol 0mg; Calcium 460mg; Fibre 0g; Sodium 20mg.

p158, Elderflower and lemon kefir (1.5ltr) Energy 411kcal/1744kJ; Protein 11.6g; Carbohydrate 92.5g, of which sugars 92.2g; Fat 1g, of which saturates 0g; Cholesterol 0mg; Calcium 417mg; Fibre 0.1g; Sodium 4mg.

p160, Coconut water kefir (1.5ltr) Energy 162kcal/685kJ; Protein 28.2g; Carbohydrate 9.7g, of which sugars 69.5g; Fat 0.8g, of which saturates 0g; Cholesterol 0mg; Calcium 292mg; Fibre 30g; Sodium 2520mg.

p162, Rejuvelac (2ltr) Energy 109kcal/457kJ; Protein 2.4g; Carbohydrate 25.5g, of which sugars 0.1g; Fat 0.5g, of which saturates 0g; Cholesterol 0mg; Calcium 4mg; Fibre 0.8g; Sodium 0mg.

p164, Fermented rhubarb fizz (1ltr) Energy 387kcal/1671kJ; Protein 1.3g; Carbohydrate 100.4g, of which sugars 99.5g; Fat 1.1g, of which saturates 0g; Cholesterol 0mg; Calcium 73mg; Fibre 0g; Sodium 22mg.

p166, Ginger beer (2ltr) Energy 690kcal/2942kJ; Protein 0.9g; Carbohydrate 182.9g, of which sugars 182.9g; Fat 0g, of which saturates 0g; Cholesterol 0mg; Calcium 51mg; Fibre 0g; Sodium 9mg.

p168, Traditional bread and beet kvass (2ltr) Energy 1520kcal/6362kJ; Protein 32g; Carbohydrate 344g, of which sugars 0g; Fat 0g, of which saturates 0g; Cholesterol 0mg; Calcium 0mg; Fibre 29.3g; Sodium 2280mg.

p170, Raspberry and pear kvass (1ltr) Energy 322kcal/1376kJ; Protein 3.2g; Carbohydrate 80.6g, of which sugars 47.1g; Fat 1.1g, of which saturates 0.2g; Cholesterol 0mg; Calcium 74mg; Fibre 6.8g; Sodium 15mg.

p172, Spiced winter kvass (1.5ltr) Energy 207kcal/881kJ; Protein 0.3g; Carbohydrate 54.2g, of which sugars 31.8g; Fat 0.4g, of which saturates 0g; Cholesterol 0mg; Calcium 21mg; Fibre 0.1g; Sodium 7mg.

p174, Fermented Nordic yulemust (2.5ltr) Energy 2084kcal/8884kJ; Protein 7.8g; Carbohydrate 543.8g, of which sugars 540.5g; Fat 1.4g, of which saturates 0.1g; Cholesterol 0mg; Calcium 225mg; Fibre 6.7g; Sodium 173mg.

p184, Simple milk kefir (1ltr) Energy 710kcal/2967kJ; Protein 37g; Carbohydrate 53.8g, of which sugars 53.7g; Fat 39.5g, of which saturates 23.6g; Cholesterol 140mg; Calcium 1276mg; Fibre 0g; Sodium 550mg.

p186, Berry kefir Energy 736kcal/3077kJ; Protein 38.2g; Carbohydrate 58.7g, of which sugars 58.6g; Fat 39.7g, of which saturates 23.7g; Cholesterol 140mg; Calcium 1303mg; Fibre 3.6g; Sodium 562mg.

p188, Homemade yogurt (300ml) Energy 276kcal/1166kJ; Protein 19.9g; Carbohydrate 27.3g, of which sugars 27.3g; Fat 10.5g, of which saturates 6.7g; Cholesterol 39mg; Calcium 700mg; Fibre 0g; Sodium 280mg.

p190, Dairy whey Energy 75kcal/314kJ; Protein 0g; Carbohydrate 17.5g, of which sugars 0g; Fat 0g, of which saturates 0g; Cholesterol 0mg; Calcium 312mg; Fibre 0g; Sodium 0mg.

p192, Fresh chive and fennel labneh Energy 390kcal/1635kJ; Protein 48.2g; Carbohydrate 13.5g, of which sugars 12g; Fat 16.2g, of which saturates 8.7g; Cholesterol 60mg; Calcium 482mg; Fibre 1g; Sodium 1127mg.

p198, Fermented cashew nut cheese Energy

1432kcal/5935kJ; Protein 44.2g; Carbohydrate 45.2g, of which sugars 11.5g; Fat 120.5g, of which saturates 23.8g; Cholesterol 0mg; Calcium 80mg; Fibre 10.7g; Sodium 627mg.

p200, Matured cashew nut cheese Energy 1461kcal/6054kJ; Protein 49.7g; Carbohydrate 45.9g, of which sugars 11.5g; Fat 121g, of which saturates 23.8g; Cholesterol 0mg; Calcium 93mg; Fibre 10.7g; Sodium 2601mg.

p202, Fermented macadamia or almond nut cheese Energy 1530kcal/6335kJ; Protein 52.8g; Carbohydrate 17.2g, of which sugars 10.5g; Fat 139.5g, of which saturates 11.1g; Cholesterol 0mg; Calcium 600mg; Fibre 0g; Sodium 624mg.

p204, Paprika and sun-dried tomato nut cheese Energy 1849kcal/7657kJ; Protein 62.1g; Carbohydrate 25.7g, of which sugars 12g; Fat 167.6g, of which saturates 14.7g; Cholesterol 0mg; Calcium 656mg; Fibre 0g; Sodium 3103mg.

p206, Garlic and herb nut cheese roll Energy 1637kcal/6788kJ; Protein 65.8g; Carbohydrate 27.3g, of which sugars 10.7g; Fat 141.4g, of which saturates 11.5g; Cholesterol 0mg; Calcium 912mg; Fibre 0.7g; Sodium 650mg.

p208, Bruna's almond cheese Energy 1581kcal/6550kJ; Protein 58.8g; Carbohydrate 23g, of which sugars 11g; Fat 140.1g, of which saturates 11.1g; Cholesterol 0mg; Calcium 618mg; Fibre 1.6g; Sodium 2598mg.

p210, Cashew yogurt Energy 256kcal/1082kJ; Protein 7.3g; Carbohydrate 45.1g, of which sugars 42.4g; Fat 6.3g, of which saturates 1g; Cholesterol 0mg; Calcium 49mg; Fibre 2.4g; Sodium 84mg.

p212, Coconut yogurt Energy 311kcal/1316kJ; Protein 8.5g; Carbohydrate 56.6g, of which sugars 53g; Fat 7.2g, of which saturates 1.2g; Cholesterol 0mg; Calcium 56mg; Fibre 2.8g; Sodium 102mg.

p214, Coconut milk kefir Energy 138kcal/587kJ; Protein 6.2g; Carbohydrate 25.4g, of which sugars 25.3g; Fat 1.6g, of which saturates 0.8g; Cholesterol 0mg; Calcium 292mg; Fibre 0g; Sodium 440mg.

p216, Raw choc cashew cheesecake Energy 5953kcal/24650kJ; Protein 113.7g; Carb 229g, of which sugars 106.4g; Fat 515.6g, of which saturates 244.5g; Cholesterol 0mg; Calcium 622mg; Fibre 94.1g; Sodium 3462mg.

p222, Sprouted wheatflour Energy 7280kcal/30440kJ; Protein 162g; Carbohydrate 1698g, of which sugars 8g; Fat 30g, of which saturates 0g; Cholesterol 0mg; Calcium 240mg; Fibre 56g; Sodium 20mg.

p224, Sourdough starter Energy 689kcal/2938kJ; Protein 16.4g; Carbohydrate 156.8g, of which sugars 5g; Fat 4g, of which saturates 0.6g; Cholesterol 0mg; Calcium 68mg; Fibre 31.2g; Sodium 3mg.

p226, Sprouted buckwheat loaf Energy 2078kcal/8671kJ; Protein 53.6g; Carbohydrate 365g, of which sugars 3.3g; Fat 54.6g, of which saturates 7g; Cholesterol 0mg; Calcium 442mg; Fibre 19.2g; Sodium 15mg.

p228, Lotta's spelt sourdough baguettes Energy 4559kcal/19372kJ; Protein 167.9g; Carbohydrate 926.5g, of which sugars 35.4g; Fat 46.2g, of which saturates 3.4g; Cholesterol 0mg; Calcium 559mg; Fibre 161.4g; Sodium 116mg.

Useful Addresses

Here are some helpful websites where I buy products and starters if I need them, or which have been recommended. Some are international. Seek out your local health and hardware stores and search online.

http://www.happykombucha.co.uk – for anything you need to get started on your fermentation adventure: jars, crockpots, fermentation lids, graters, pounders, as well as various starters and cultures.

http://www.kefirshop.co.uk – for good-quality kefir starters and a few other starters.

http://www.tree-harvest.com – for good-quality organic raw nuts and seeds for your nut cheese, as well as herbs and spices.

http://www.ikea.co.uk – well-priced kilner-style glass jars.

http://www.lakeland.co.uk – for utensils, jars, bowls, muslin cloths and fermentation lids; they also sell a range of graters, processors and blenders.

http://www.madmillie.com – utensils for cheese-making and nut cheese-making, as well as useful products for other kinds of fermentation.

http://leparfait.co.uk – supplier of quality kilner-style and other jars.

http://www.sauerkrautpots.com – a producer of traditional crockpots.

http://www.culturesforhealth.com – for equipment and cultures.

http://lehmans.com – for fermentation equipment and more.

http://perfectpickler.com – for fermentation equipment and more.

http://www.wholesomesupplies.com.au – for fermentation jars.

http://www.britishgut.org and http://humanfoodproject.com/americangut/ – a scientific project looking at people's microbiome. If you want to know what your microbiome looks like, you can participate.

Bibliography

Balfour Sartor, R. (2008). Microbial Influences in Inflammatory Bowel Diseases. Gastroenterology. 134(2); 577–594.

Campbell McBride, N. (2010). Gut and Psychology Syndrome, Natural Treatment for. Cambridge. Mediform Publishing.

Chilton, S. N., Burton, J. P., & Reid, G. (2015). Inclusion of Fermented Foods in Food Guides Around the World. Nutrients. 7(1); 390–404.

Cho, K. M., Math, R.K., Islam, S. M., Lim, W. J., Hong, S. Y., Kim, J. M., Yun, M. G., Cho, J. J., & Yun, H. D. (2009). Biodegradation of chlorpyrifos by lactic acid bacteria during kimchi fermentation. Journal of Agricultural and Food Chemistry. 57(5); 1882–1889.

Chung, H., Pamp, S. J., Hill, J. A., Surana, N. K., Edelman, S. M., Troy, E. B., & Kasper, D. L. (2012). Gut immune maturation depends on colonization with a host-specific microbiot-cell.149(7); 1578–1593.

Cooper, P., Bolton, K. D., Velaphi, S., de Groot, N., Emady-Azar, S., Pecquet, S., & Steenhout, P. (2016). Early benefits of a starter formula enriched in prebiotics and probiotics on the gut microbiota of healthy infants born to HIV+ mothers: a randomized double-blind controlled trial. Clinical Medicine Insights. Pediatrics. 10; 119–130.

Den Besten, G., van Eunen, K., Groen, A. K., Venema, K., Reijngoud, D.-J., & Bakker, B. M. (2013). The role of short-chain fatty acids in the interplay between diet, gut microbiota, and host energy metabolism. Journal of Lipid Research. 54(9); 2325–2340.

Fuentes, M.C., Lajo, T., Carrión, J. M., & Cuñé, J. (2013). Cholesterol-lowering efficacy of Lactobacillus plantarum CECT 7527, 7528 and 7529 in hypercholesterolaemic adults. British Journal of Nutrition. 109; 1866–1872.

Greger, Michael (2015). How not to Die – Discover the foods scientifically proven to prevent disease. New York. Flatiron Books.

Hemalatha, S., Platel, K. & Srinivasan, K. (2007). Influence of germination and fermentation on bioaccessibility of zinc and iron from food grains. European Journal of Clinical Nutrition. 61(3); 342–348.

Jovanovic-Malinovska, R., Kuzmanova, S., & Winkelhausen, E. (2012). Oligosaccharide profile in fruits and vegetables as sources of prebiotics and functional foods.

Katz Ellix, Sandor (2012). The Art of Fermentation – an in-depth exploration of essential concepts and processes from around the world. USA. Chelsea Green Publishing.

Kim, Y., Keogh, J., & Clifton, P. (2018). Probiotics, prebiotics, symbiotics and insulin sensitivity. Nutrition Research Reviews. 31(1); 35–51.

Krajmalnik-Brown, R., Ilhan, Z.-E., Kang, D.-W., & DiBaise, J. K. (2012). Effects of gut microbes on nutrient absorption and energy regulation.nutrition in clinical practice: official publication of the American Society for Parenteral and Enteral Nutrition. 27(2); 201–214.

Minot, S., Sinha, R., Chen, J., Li, H., Keilbaugh, S. A., Wu, G. D., & Bushman, F. D. (2011). The human gut virome: Inter-individual variation and dynamic response to diet. Genome Research. 21(10); 1616–1625.

Mosley, M. (2017). The Clever Guts Diet. London. Short Books.

Mueller, N. T., Bakacs, E., Combellick, J., Grigoryan, Z., & Dominguez-Bello, M. G. (2014). The infant microbiome development: mom matters. Trends in molecular medicine. 21(2); 109–117.

O'Mahony, S. M., Clarke, G., Borre, Y., Dinan, T., & Cryan, J., (2015). Serotonin, tryptophan metabolism and the brain-gut-microbiome axis. Behavioural Brain Research. 277; 32–48.

Panduro, A., Riviera-Iniguez, I., Sepulveda-Villegas, M., & Roman, S. (2017). Genes, emotions and gut macrobiota: the next frontier for the gastroenterologist. World Journal of Gastroenterology. 23(7); 303–304.

Pannaraj, P. S., Li, F., Cerini, C., Bender, J. M., Yang, S., Rollie, A., Adisetiyo, H., Zabih, S., Linsec, P. J., Bittinger, K., Bailey, A., Bushman, F. D., Sleasman, J. W., & Aldrovandi, G. M. (2017). Association between breast milk bacterial communities and establishment and development of the infant gut microbiome. Jama Pediatrics. 171(7); 647–654.

Paramithiotisf, S. (2017). Lactic Acid Fermentation of Fruits and Vegetables. Portland. CRC Press.

Prescott, S. L., Logan, A. C. (2017). The Secret Life of your Microbiome. Gabriola Island. New Society Publishers.

Schwenk, Donna (2013). Cultured Food for Life. USA. Hay House.

Sender, R., Fuchs, S., & Milo, R. (2016). Revised estimates for the number of human and bacteria cells in the body. Plos Biology. 14(8); e1002533.

Left: Simple lemon water kefir made with coconut sugar and molasses, *see page 154.*

Shetty, S. A., Hugenholtz, F., Lahti, L., Smidt, H., & de Vos, W. (2017). Intestinal microbiome landscaping: insight in community assemblage and implications for microbial modulation strategies. FEMS Microbiology Reviews. 41(2); 182–199.

Siervo, M., Lara, J., Ogbonmwan, I., & Mathers, J. C. (2013). Inorganic nitrate and beetroot juice supplementation reduces blood pressure in adults: a systematic review and meta-analysis. Journal of Nutrition. 143(6); 818–826.

Singh, R. K., Chang, H., Liao, W., Yan, D., Lee, K. M., Ucmak, D., Wong, K., Abrouk, M., Farahnik, B., Nakamura, M., Zhu, T. H., & Bhutani, T. (2017). Influence of diet on the gut microbime and implications for human health. Journal of Translational Medicine. 15(1); 73.

Stout, M. J., Conlon, B., Landeau, M., Lee, I., Bower, C., Zhao, Q., & Mysorekar, I. U. (2013). Identification of intracellular bacteria in the basal plate of the human placenta in term and preterm gestations. American Journal of Obstetrics and Gynecology. 208(3); 226.e1–226.e7.

Sunagawa, S., Blottiere, H., Jensen, B., Oresic, M., Pedersen, H., Gudmundsdottir, V., Nielsen, H., Plichta, D., Hellgren, L., Brix, S., Brunak, S., Hyotylainen, T., Oresic, M., Mattila, I., Poho, P., Nielsen, T., Arumugam, M., Hansen, T., Pedersen, O., Jensen, B., Holm, J., Kristiansen, K., Wang, J., Forslund, K., Hildebrand, F., Sunagawa, S., Bork, P., Raes, J., Falony, G., Vieira-Silva, S., Prifti, E., Le Chatelier, E., Levenez, F., Dore, J., Ehrlich, S., Trost, K., & Jorgensen, T. (2016). Human gut microbes impact host serum metabolome and insulin sensitivity, Nature. 535 (7612); 376.

Thaiss, C. A., Itav, S., Rothchild, D., Meijer, M., Levy, M., Moresi, C., Dohnalova, L., Braveman, S., Rozin, S., Malitsky, S., Dori-Bachash, M., Kuperman, Y., Biton, I., Gertler, A., Harmelin, A., Shapiro, H., Halpern, Z., Ahorini, A., Segal, E., & Elinav, E. (2016). Persistent Microbiome alterations modulate the rate of post dieting weight regain. Nature, 540; 544–551.

Wiczkowski, W., Szawara-Nowak, D., & Romaszko, J. (2016). The impact of red cabbage fermentation on bioavailability of anthocyanins and antioxidant capacity of human plasma. Food Chem. 190, 730–740.

Wong, J., de Souza, R., Kendall, C., Emam, E., & Jenkins, D. (2006). Colonic health: fermentation and short chain fatty acids. Journal of Clinical Gastroenteroly; 40(3); 235–243.

Index

Acknowledgements

Åsa Linéa Simonsson is a Nutritionist and Naturopath, with over 20 years of experience working in the natural health and beauty industry. After a BSc in Psychology, she trained and worked in her native Sweden as a nurse, before moving to the UK, where she set up a successful business manufacturing and selling natural plant-based beauty products, and training as a Naturopath. Åsa sees clients in her practice in London as well as working as a lecturer at the College of Naturopathic Medicine. She is passionate about healthy eating and especially plant-based food. She is a raw food chef at Restore Retreat, and holds regular workshops on fermentation and healthy food. Her website is http://www.lineanutrition.co.uk and instagram @nordic.nutrition.

For Howard, Jonah and Elsa

Published by Lorenz Books
an imprint of Anness Publishing Ltd
www.lorenzbooks.com; info@anness.com

Publisher: Joanna Lorenz
Photography: William Shaw
Food styling: Heather Whinney and Åsa Simonsson
Design: Adelle Mahoney
Nutritional consultant: Clare Emery
Index: Marie Lorimer

Although the advice and information in this book are believed to be accurate and true at the time of going to press, neither the author nor the publisher can accept any legal responsibility or liability for any errors or omissions that may have been made nor for any loss, harm or injury that comes about from following this book.

 A CIP catalogue record for this book is available from the British Library.

NOTES FOR THE READER

Fermentation is a natural process and results may vary; please read the first chapters carefully for general advice on ingredients, equipment, hygiene and safety. Glass jars and bottles very rarely explode during fermentation but it has been known to happen.

The book is not intended as a substitute for professional diagnosis. Any person with a condition requiring medical attention should consult a doctor or qualified practitioner.

For all recipes, quantities are given in both metric and imperial measures. Follow one set of measures, but not a mixture, because they are not interchangeable. Standard spoon and cup measures are level. 1 tsp = 5ml, 1 tbsp = 15ml, 1 cup = 250ml/9fl oz. Australian standard tablespoons are 20ml; Australian readers should use 3 tsp in place of 1 tbsp for measuring small quantities. American pints are 16fl oz/2 cups; American readers should use 20fl oz/2½ cups in place of 1 pint when measuring liquids.

The nutritional analysis given for each recipe is calculated per total weight (or per portion when specified). The analysis does not include optional ingredients.